D0984836

evolutionary love
and the Ravages of Greed

Adam Crabtree

Suite 300 - 990 Fort St
Victoria, BC, V8V 3K2
Canada

www.friesenpress.com

ISBN
978-1-5255-0967-4 (Hardcover)
978-1-5255-0968-1 (Paperback)
978-1-5255-0969-8 (eBook)

1. PHILOSOPHY

Distributed to the trade by The Ingram Book Company

Acknowledgements

I would like to recognize first the important role played by Jim and Christina Grote in the writing and publishing of this book. They have encouraged me at various stages of my work and offered important feedback on the content. They have also promoted its publication with moral and financial support.

Numerous other people have provided valuable responses to my writing as it progressed. I would like to make special mention of Robert Corrington, who encouraged and inspired me in various ways. I would also like to thank Matthew Ahern, Pam Kramer, Julia Mossbridge, Karin Porter, and Eric Robertson for reading the manuscript in the course of its evolution. A special word of thanks goes to my son, Andrew Crabtree, whose philosophical insights and editorial input have been invaluable. Finally, I am most grateful to Mike Murphy, who encouraged my early investigation of Peirce and expressed strong emotional support for my attempt to say something significant about love.

Table of Contents

Introduction

Greed dominates our world today. We see it at every turn in its societal, political, institutional, and individual forms. We sense that greed means a lack of love. But just how greed relates to love and how love can counteract its effects may not be all that clear. Because of its powerful influence in our world, I offer this book as an attempt to fathom the essential meaning of greed and, more importantly, to explore the fundamental power of love to end its dominance.

In the Netflix series *House of Cards*, the unscrupulous protagonist, Francis Underwood, tells us that greed is either greed for money or greed for power. He despises those who exercise greed for mere money, which he considers a base and less intelligent form of greed. Underwood sees the core meaning of greed as the attainment of power and is convinced that if one concentrates his or her efforts on accumulating power, money will take care of itself. He also believes those who concentrate on money narrow their perspective and thereby become vulnerable to manipulation. The view of greed in popular culture tends to emphasize the money aspect, as we can see for instance, in the CNN series on *The Eighties*, which describes that period as the decade of greed and the Wall Street manipulator as the wizard of greed. Those infected by greed for money, whether they be rich or poor, reduce the world to economics. Those who espouse greed for power reduce the world to politics. I believe Underwood's view of the core nature of greed is closer to the truth. Greed is the insatiable and unrestrained desire for *any* means of self-enhancement.

Greed for power can take many forms, from a despotic leader's domination of a country to a petty mobster dominating a neighborhood. The classic film *Key Largo* includes a scene that portrays naked greed in a striking way. Rocco

(Edward G. Robinson) is a mobster of the worst kind, sadistic and ruthless. Frank (Humphrey Bogart) is a veteran and a hero, just returned from the war. James Temple (Lionel Barrymore) is the owner of the hotel taken over by Rocco and his thugs. The following dialogue occurs when Temple asks Rocco what he wants for himself:

> Frank: He knows what he wants—don't you, Rocco?
>
> Rocco: Sure.
>
> Temple: What's that?
>
> Frank: Tell him, Rocco.
>
> Rocco: Well, I want . . ..
>
> Frank: He wants more. Don't you, Rocco?
>
> Rocco: That's *it*! *More*, that's right! I want *more*!
>
> Temple: You'll never get enough, will you, Rocco?
>
> Rocco: Well, I never have! No, I guess I won't!

Greed is insatiable. Whether one seeks power, influence, money, land, consumer goods, food, sex, fame, preferential treatment, control—greed always wants more.

I see the domination of the world by greed today as a defect in the exercise of love. In fact, I describe greed precisely in those terms, as the unconstrained desire for any sort of enrichment. For that reason, it is impossible to fully expose greed in our world and explore the possibilities of opposing its dominance without first talking about *love* in its essential meaning.

> Philosophy, when just escaping from its golden pupa-skin, mythology, proclaimed the great evolutionary agency of the universe to be Love.
>
> —Charles Sanders Peirce[1]

The great American philosopher, Charles Sanders Peirce, believed that love was central to the existence and functioning of the universe. He saw one kind of love in particular as the driving force behind the development and fulfillment of all things. This is what Peirce called "evolutionary love."

I first spoke publicly about this idea in 2012 at an Integral Transformative Practice workshop in San Francisco. I had been studying Peirce's work and became intrigued by a little treatise he wrote in 1893 for a periodical called the *Monist*. He gave it the striking title "Evolutionary Love," and from its opening words, he adopted a tone very different from that of his other writings. It feels like a demand for the reader's attention, a summons to pay heed to a message of crucial importance. I felt drawn to the powerful flow of ideas, and as I read, a compelling vision took shape for me. The more I was immersed in the piece, the more puzzled I became that this remarkable manifesto had almost completely escaped the notice of those engaged in exploring the fundamental nature of the world and the meaning of human life.

If you had Googled the term "evolutionary love" in 2012, you would have found few responses: only direct references to Peirce's article and citations of that piece by philosophical scholars. Now, five years later, it is popping up all over the place. There seems to be a sense that something of great value is hidden in the conjunction of those two words, something that responds to the current urgent need to understand, on the deepest possible level, the disturbances that trouble the modern human community.

After that talk in 2012, I developed my initial ideas and made them available in certain online scholarly repositories of current academic work. Most recently, I have referred to evolutionary love in the final chapter of my book, *Memoir of a Trance Therapist*, and in a chapter in *Beyond Physicalism*.[2] In the meantime, I became convinced that evolutionary love deserves a more thorough treatment than I have given it so far.

In Peirce's article, penned more than a century ago, he presented certain novel, richly evocative ideas. He argued that love is a philosophical principle that is fundamental to understanding not only human interactions and strivings but also the very constitution of the universe. Peirce, however, introduced a new perspective on the ancient theme, presenting love as the engine that drives all evolution: human and cosmic. He defined this love as "the ardent impulse to fulfill another's highest impulse" (CP 6, 289), which, taken in its broadest meaning, is the desire that loved beings reach their greatest possible development, the fullest actualization of their potentials. Put in more modern language, it is the unconditional desire that the object of love achieve its greatest possible evolutionary fulfillment. He contrasts this view of evolutionary growth with the strife of the Darwinian approach, which explains everything through natural selection and survival of the fittest, and the mechanistic view of determinism, which posits a world with a completely predetermined future. Peirce recognized that both approaches make valid contributions to our understanding of the mechanisms of evolution, but he insisted that something more was needed to offer a full explanation for evolution as it actually functions in our world. To provide an adequate vision of evolution, he introduced the notion of a beneficent, foundational evolutionary force, a selfless love that—following the lead of the Gospel of John—he called *agape*, in contrast with the self-focused love characterized by desire that the Greeks called *eros*.

For Peirce, evolution was not merely a matter of biology. Based on a profound metaphysical view of reality, which he derived from a scientifically grounded empiricism, he held that everything evolves. Furthermore, he held that human beings have a unique position in nature, being able to contribute consciously to their own evolutionary advance through participation in evolutionary love and possessing the power to make free choices that have real effects on the evolution of the universe.

Disappointingly, Peirce did not develop this striking evolutionary panorama as far as one might wish. It is my intention to elaborate and expand upon Peirce's vision, suggesting a view of the nature and direction of the evolving cosmos that has practical consequences for the determination of right action for individuals and human communities.

In this book, I propose a view of love that can be expressed in three ideas: 1) Two loves form the foundation for cosmic and human evolution: benevolent love (*agape*) and desire love (*eros*). 2) Our dealings with each other and the world involve a mixture of these two loves, and if our actions are to honor the fundamental nature of things, benevolent love must be given primacy over *eros* in our moral choices. 3) If that primacy is violated, and *eros* dominates, the result is a greed for power or wealth that corrupts basic values and blocks the great project of humankind: the promotion of evolutionary advancement and the discovery of truth.

Part One: Love

Chapter 1: Love

In his groundbreaking article on evolutionary love, Charles Sanders Peirce chose the Greek word *agape* as the most appropriate vehicle for his novel concept. Although *agape* is an ancient term, Peirce thought that as used in the New Testament, especially in the Gospel of John, *agape* indicated a revolutionary interpretation of love in its deepest meaning: the benevolent and unconditional desire for the fullest possible realization of the potentials, or latent capacities, of the loved one. Peirce believed that the exploration of *agape* holds the key to understanding the evolution of the universe and the purpose of human life. I have decided to follow Peirce and use the word *agape* to refer to evolutionary love in all its aspects.

In its foundational meaning, *agape* is a primordial enabling condition necessary for the existence of an evolving world. It is the engine of evolution, urging every existing thing to realize its potentials to the greatest extent possible. It is the driver and sustainer of all evolutionary development, both cosmic and human.

In its social meaning, *agape* is a central fact of human moral life. As human beings, we have a unique relation to *agape*. We can feel what *agape* is, not merely through being objects of the agapic love that pervades the universe but also as beings capable of the subjective feeling of *agape* and as participating agents of its power. We can feel agapic love toward all things and make deliberate choices about how we are going to interact with those things in accordance with that love, and this gives us a direct sense of *agape* that is unavailable to any other beings.

Looked at from our unique vantage point, we see that *agape* is:

- *Benevolent* love: a human emotion and intention that wishes well to all

- *Unconditional* love: an attitude characterized by the recognition that loved ones are free and self-determining, a gift given without preconditions, without any claim of merit, and without expectations for future actions

- *Empathic* love: a sentiment of oneness with others and a feeling of commonality with all, which is the basis for relationships, personal and communal, and is expressed in feelings of compassion

- *Non-possessive* love: an attitude of non-interference regarding others' life decisions

- *Respectful* love: an appreciation of others, in all their uniqueness, in their rich potentials (both realized and unrealized), and in their unfathomable depths as creatures rooted in the mysterious ground of nature

Agape is fundamentally benevolent. It consists of an abundance of goodwill directed to loved ones. It is a well-wishing love. The benefit it wishes is the greatest possible evolutionary advance for the beloved persons or entities and their complete fulfillment.

Although evolutionary love arises from the ineffable wellspring of the universe, it is also something that human beings experience subjectively. It is instinctual in us in our capacity as intelligent, individual manifestations of the one primal source of love. We experience the objects of our love—other people and the environment in which we are immersed—as separate from us. But we and they are actually part of a great continuum of being that includes everything in the manifesting cosmos.

When someone is loved agapically, that person finds no justification for the love and, if reflective, is taken aback, for the love given is unmerited. It is a mysterious gift, received without warrant, and, as such, may be called "grace." The loved one has the feeling of being loved not because of what he or she is here and now but for the latent potentials waiting to be actualized.

Agape is unconditional. Agapic love is not given on some precondition that has been met by the loved one. *Agape* is given precisely when the loved one has not achieved what he or she can achieve. By the very exercise of *agape*, the lover seeks to support the conditions needed for the realization of those potentials. *Agape* is also unconditional in that it is not given with any expectation of what the loved one will do in return. No strings are attached. It is not given on the condition that loved ones will make decisions that are in accord with the lover's inclinations. *Agape* desires that loved ones freely determine their own future and make their own decisions about their actions. The lover has no say about what his/her fulfillment consists in and what his/her actions should be. So, agapic lovers should not be taken by surprise when loved ones act in a way that the lover disapproves. *Agape* does not require the lover to subscribe to all actions taken by loved ones; both lover and loved one remain free to make their own moral judgments.

By arising from a common source, the very wellspring of the universe, every existing thing is continuous with every other existing thing. This manifests in the feeling of empathy, an instinctive care and concern for all of creation. In human relations, this empathic love is felt as compassion.

The agapic lover does not want to possess the loved being, in the sense of taking ownership. The act of possession would immediately disrespect the loved one, for it would interfere with the free and full realization of the loved one's potentials, of those possibilities for growth that are waiting to be brought into existence. By possessing a love object, the lover would interfere with it and block its ability to freely develop into whatever it will be.

Agape has respect for the loved one. This respect is not based on the loved one's accomplishments but on the potentials that are yet to be realized. Of course, the agapic lover may have some ideas, of a general kind, about the sort of outcomes those potentials may produce (the potentials of an infant, for instance, do not resemble those of an acorn). Nevertheless, the motivation for *agape* is not to bring about specific forms of actualization.

If love is so fundamental, why are we constantly confronted by hatred and greed in the doings of the world around us? And why must we struggle to fan the sparks of this love we find within ourselves to approach the world with loving sentiments? We need to find out about these things by looking deeper into what love is, how it operates in our personal and social lives, and how it enters our moral decisions. To do that, we must look at another form of love—*eros*.

Eros

For Peirce, Christian *agape* had replaced the Greek philosophers' *eros* as the ground of being. *Eros* was the term employed in the Platonic philosophical tradition to describe the love that urges the individual to the attainment of divine qualities of perfection. It was used to describe the desire for spiritual growth of all kinds and believed to provide the highest motivations for human moral choices. It was seen as the passionate desire that connects human beings with each other and the world around us. In Peirce's view, although superseded by *agape*, *eros* still has an essential, albeit secondary, role in the process of human and cosmic evolution.

Eros regards the loved one as valuable and wants to be enriched by that value. It is thus at the service of the lover and the lover's destiny. *Eros* is the love that seeks to be enhanced by the loved one, in that the lover is motivated by desire for the beauty seen in the beloved and experiences a longing to make that beauty his or her own. In this way, the *eros*-driven lover is seeking the means to evolve, to develop the self, through opportunities for engagement with beautiful and desirable objects.

This meaning of *eros* is the one I use throughout this book. In Western culture, *eros* has come to be equated with sexual feelings and sexual encounters; that is not the meaning of *eros* here. Rather, I define *eros* in the much broader terms that originate in the Platonic tradition of philosophy. In that tradition, sex is only one manifestation of *eros*. The full meaning of the term sees *eros* as desire-love, the longing of the lover to be enhanced though the encounter with a love object that embodies something of value for the lover, something the lover wants to absorb and be enriched by.

Enrichment of the lover through this sort of *eros* can come in many forms. We can be enriched physically, emotionally, mentally, or spiritually. Physically, our bodies can be enriched by food, exercise, body-enhancing activities and beautifications, or sex; and our physical senses can give us powerful experiences of visual art or music. We can be enriched emotionally though our interactions with people in a variety of relationships, from casual to intimate. This enrichment can involve an enhancement of mood, increase of confidence, growth in optimism, or joy in living. Mental enrichment occurs in learning situations that make us better informed, more skilled, or wiser. Spiritual enrichment puts us in touch with a broader and deeper sense of the beauty that shines forth in everything and with the meaning of the world and human life.

In his discussions of love of knowledge, we encounter the few references that Peirce makes to the positive function of *eros* for the individual and the human community. His writings, he tells us, are for people who *want to find out.* He has no desire for followers, however, writing that "people who want philosophy ladled out to them can go elsewhere. There are philosophical soup shops at every corner" (CP 1.11), Peirce laments that the "present infantile condition of philosophy" is that those who pursue it are so seldom "animated by true scientific *Eros*" but are often motivated by already formed philosophical or theological ideas and animated by "a spirit …radically unfitting them for the task of scientific investigation" (CP 1:620).

Enrichment through *eros* contributes to personal growth and fulfillment. The different forms of enrichment come in our interactions with others, and, as we shall see, even in encounters with the rest of the natural world. In the love drive of *eros*, we feel an urge, a compulsion, to evolve, to grow, to become what we are capable of being. For that reason, we seek out *eros* encounters of all kinds. This desire for enrichment can be felt as a kind of hunger that longs for satisfaction. The hunger and seeking out is natural and crucial to our evolutionary development. However, experience tells us that in the process of trying to satisfy that hunger, we can lose perspective. We may not foresee the results of our actions. The desire for enrichment through *eros* may reach an intensity that clouds our awareness of the implications of those actions for the loved one with whom we are engaged.

Particularly in *eros* encounters with other people, we need to maintain an appropriate awareness of what we are doing. Personal *eros*-driven love seeks a response and can involve a certain objectification of the loved one. In personal relationships, reciprocity on the part of the loved one is sought, and as long as the lover does not seek to possess (in the sense of own or control), the love object remains intact and free. Loss of this perspective leads to trouble.

Agape and *Eros*

So, in our lives, we experience two fundamentally distinct kinds of love: (1) *agape*, an appreciative and selfless love of other people or things for their own sake and (2) *eros*, a love that seeks the lover's personal enrichment through the loved person or entity. Agapic love is a benevolent and unconditional love that is concerned only with the development and fulfillment of the loved one. *Eros*-driven love desires interaction with loved ones for their ability to fulfill the lover. *Agape* is unselfish; *eros* is self-serving. *Agape* is characterized by overflowing abundance; *eros* by need. *Agape* is ecological (wanting to preserve nature's fullest unimpeded outpourings); *eros* is utilitarian (desiring to enjoy or exploit nature for personal/societal gain).

Agape is selfless. This is true not merely because it does not seek self-enhancement but also because *agape* does not originate in the self. It is cosmic in origin, and while we can participate in it and channel it, we cannot take credit for it. We do not create *agape* and do not own it, but we have the privilege of being centers of its conscious manifestation in the world. In this way, we are agents in both cosmic and human evolution.

Although *agape* is the fundamental driver of evolution, *eros* plays a crucial role in the evolutionary process. *Agape* grounds evolution in the universe; *eros* is the means through which, on a concrete level, evolution takes place. Through *eros*-driven encounters, beings experience greater fulfillment of their potentials and move forward on their evolutionary path.

Eros is selfish not because it involves a narrow egotism but because it is the means by which we build and grow our selves. We seek encounters that will advance our evolution as persons. *Eros* creates a hunger for opportunities to develop our potentials and capacities and become what we can be. The distinction between *agape* and *eros* is critical to any full understanding of the human experience of love. I intend to explore that distinction throughout this book.

Moral Choices

The interplay of *agape* and *eros* informs the whole of human moral life. All the troubles that occur in relationships—between individuals, between individuals and their surrounding world, and between groups and their social environment—arise from the flawed interplay of these two loves. The destructiveness and devastating lack of respect that we see in the world today are due to the lack of balance between these two forces. Both kinds of love are essential to the world's growth and evolution, but only when they are in balance can the natural and social environments in which we live prosper. In today's world, both environments are in danger.

Examining the nature of the love found in friendship illustrates how the two loves combine in human interactions. I love a friend because of the valuable contributions that my contacts with him introduce into my life. He likes me, and this enhances my feelings of confidence and self-worth. He is interesting and intelligent, and his friendship deepens my understanding of the world and life. In his actions, he exemplifies many virtues, and I emulate him and desire to be like him, to become virtuous myself. He speaks honestly to me about his impressions of me, and this makes me think seriously about what I am like and how I might be better. Through my interactions with him, I grow stronger and more authentic in my actions and more successful in my social encounters. Also, he makes me laugh and feel greater joy in living. These are all reasons I seek out my friend, to grow and develop my potentials on many levels. These are the elements of *eros* in my love for my friend.

But I also feel agapic love toward my friend. I frequently find myself feeling delight in his personal growth. I wish him well in all his undertakings. I support him in his projects. I see the many ways he has evolved in his intellectual, emotional, and spiritual life, and I want him to continue to become the person he desires to be. These are the agapic elements of my love for my friend.

Agape Must Be Primary

Virtually all love relationships involve a combination of *eros* and *agape*. In our moral decisions, that is, our decisions about what actions we will take, we must reach a balance between the two, while recognizing the principle that *agape* has primacy over *eros*-driven love in all human choices. This principle, in turn, is based on two facts. First, while agapic love is the primal force behind all evolution, *eros*-driven love is the mechanism by which evolution works itself out through concrete interactions within the world. Second, in human affairs, *eros*-driven love is concerned with the growth of the lover, and, as such, has no internal constraints. Left to its own devices, *eros* may continue to seek its own enrichment and, if unrestrained, can devour the love object to the point of destroying it. Unrestrained *eros* is the essence of greed, the self-centered hunger for power and wealth, and greed has no concern for the welfare of its desired loved one. *Agape* provides the natural restraining influence on *eros* needed to ensure that the loved one is not harmed. Put another way, *agape* is the conscience of *eros*. *Eros* wishes to enrich itself through its relationship with another, and if *eros* becomes dominant over *agape*, love tips toward greed.[3]

The principle of the primacy of the agapic may also be discussed in terms of how *agape* affects the lover. What, if anything, does the lover gain? The lover's gain comes through being affected by the evocative power in the depth of the loved one. Rather than engaging with surface qualities, the lover encounters an excess in the loved one, a surplus, a something *more* that puts the lover in touch with the depths of nature in which the loved one is rooted and thereby creates a feeling of awe in response to the loved one. When the lover is affected in that way, he or she engages with something transcendent, something that arises from a reality beyond both lover and loved one. This experience creates a unique feeling of pleasure. Nevertheless, that pleasure is not the motive for the giving of agapic love but a fortunate consequence of it.

In human affairs, *agape* and *eros* exist in constant interplay. Moral decisions involve determining how to apply the principle of the primacy of agapic love in a world where *eros* is continually active. Moral decisions made according to the principle of the primacy of *agape* are not necessarily simple and, in some cases, may be reached only with great difficulty. All moral decisions are challenging because of the immense complexity of real-life circumstances.

If I attend a lecture by a philosopher that I admire, I hope to be intellectually enriched by her. I hope to be stimulated by the philosopher's ideas, deepened in my grasp of the scope of the problems of philosophy, and confirmed in certain tentative philosophical ideas that I am developing. Insofar as I have these expectations, what I experience is an *eros*-driven love: I hope that I will personally be enhanced by her and become a better philosopher and a better person.

At a party, a young man meets a charismatic, successful businessman. The young man feels attracted to the businessman's energy, the feeling of power and confidence that radiates from him. He feels drawn to talk to him, to get to know him, and perhaps to establish a connection that could lead to interesting and satisfying employment. He hopes to enrich his life through the growth of confidence that such an association could bring, to say nothing of the financial rewards. In this way, he experiences feelings of *eros* regarding the businessman and hopes the potential connection will move him forward on his evolutionary path.

Rarely, if ever, is love simply *agape* or simply *eros*. My *eros*-driven desire for enrichment by my admired philosopher is not without elements of *agape*. I appreciate her and want her to continue developing professionally and as a person, becoming ever more of what she can be through her life experiences.

In any case, on the level of human love and the moral life, everything is in the service of evolution. With *agape,* we desire and support the loved one's evolution. With *eros*, the lover seeks his or her own evolutionary advance. On the level of cosmic love, *agape* is the force that pushes the evolution of the universe forward. *Eros* is the energy employed by all things to advance themselves, individually or collectively, along their evolutionary path. To understand this, it is necessary to look deeper at the nature of evolution.

Evolution

Agape is the foundation for evolution. This is why Peirce called *agape* evolutionary love. Evolutionary love leaves the object of love free to choose its own evolutionary path. It imposes no specific goal on the love object but rather supports the process by which it makes its own choices. The love object remains free, while evolutionary love gently urges it toward its own unique fulfillment. Evolutionary love is not given because of merit, and it attaches no strings or conditions to its support. The evolutionary lover has no expectations and demands nothing for him or herself. It is fully unconditional love.

In terms of our present discussion, Darwin's view of evolution is based exclusively on the operation of *eros*. For Darwin, the evolving organism carries out actions solely for its own benefit and growth, as well as that of its family and progeny. Peirce introduced his concept of *agape* into the understanding of evolution to correct what he considered this serious inadequacy in Darwin's approach (as well as that of those who take a deterministic view of evolution). His evolutionary vision of *agape* does not merely introduce a new element into the Darwinist mix. Rather, it restructures the entire framework of evolution. Here *agape* is held to be the condition that makes evolution possible. *Agape* is its cosmic foundation, and *eros* is an active dynamic in service of the purposes of *agape*.[4]

After Darwin made his discoveries relating to biological evolution in *The Origin of Species*, published in 1859, many began to apply his principles to other areas, including human culture and social norms. Peirce, however, went further, contending that evolution is not limited to the biological or sociological but is a primal characteristic of all that exists. Everything evolves, and everything evolves in a direction. Peirce said, "evolution is nothing more or less than the working out of a definite end,"[5] and any general evolutionary theory must account for this fact. This is not to say it is possible to show precisely what that direction consists of but that the world is becoming increasingly definite. Over eons, the universe is working toward a goal, the gradual actualization of the potentials that exist within it. In agreement with Peirce,[6] I believe that at the beginning of the world, before anything existed, there was nothing—not a pure nothingness but a nothingness teeming with possibilities. Over the ages since the beginning, those potentials have been gradually activated, becoming real, existing things that are in constant change—evolving.

In the coming into being of the cosmos, each potentiality develops from an indeterminate state, progresses to become a determinate possibility, and then, at last, emerges as an existent thing. The gradual actualization of potentials and the fulfillment of possibilities is what evolution is all about.

An acorn that falls from an oak tree already has a certain determinateness, a set of inherent possibilities that mean it will become an oak tree and not a white pine.[7] But this determinateness is not complete, for the variety of possible, specific oak trees that could come into existence from a particular acorn is virtually unlimited and is influenced by many factors. For example, the actualization of the possibilities in a tree occurs under the influence of the environment in which it finds itself, so that a sapling growing in a time of prolonged drought may become stunted.

Agapic love provides the direction for the evolutionary process at work in the cosmos. That overarching goal of the cosmos and of every evolving thing is to realize its potentials to the greatest possible extent. This universal goal gently draws the evolving being forward and at the same time leaves it free to make its own choices about the means it will use to forward its growth. Peirce did not believe the goal of evolution was set out beforehand by God or the Absolute. He believed the direction of evolutionary change, both immediate and in the long run, is provided by the evolving entities themselves, who constantly infuse the element of free, spontaneous choice into the process.

Here the notion of *telos* or goal is key. Telos is central in Peirce's philosophy of mind. For Peirce, mind is that which acts with a purpose, seeking a goal or telos. Since all life acts purposively, all life is telos-directed. Indeed, for Peirce, life and mind are synonyms. Without an overall telos, there would be nothing but chaos.

This notion of telos is absent from Darwinian and deterministic approaches to evolution. But for Peirce, any approach that denies the reality of teleology in the world fails to explain the facts of experience. The same position was recently put forward by philosopher Thomas Nagel. He says evidence suggests that the psychophysical reductionism held so commonly today has failed and that "principles of a different kind are also at work in the history of nature, principles of the growth of order that are in their logical form teleological rather than mechanistic."[8]

The teleological universe progresses toward a desired outcome; it moves forward under the guidance of a purpose or purposes. But the universe moves forward by means of innumerable goal-driven increments as well. Each thing is constantly setting goals for the next moment of existence, adopting a telos, a goal, that then lures it forward to the form it will take at the next moment. These teloi, determined only partially by present circumstances, lead to a new moment, at which point a new goal is chosen, and the process continues. Not being fully determined by present conditions, the outcome reveals an element of cosmic freedom at work in the constantly evolving streams of goals that Peirce calls developmental teleology.[9] This means the universe is an advancing flow of continuously shifting mini-goals, which at the same time are converging on an ideal goal in the distant future: the fulfillment of the universe.

Because this universe forms a continuum, from its beginning to all things that we know of today and all that will come to be known in the future, everything is connected to everything else. It is because of this connectedness that Peirce spoke of a sympathy that pervades all things, a sympathy by which all things "sense" everything else, not through what we call the five senses but through a more generalized sense of contact or communion. All creation has this sympathy, but human beings have a special capacity to become conscious of this feeling, to reach an understanding of the nature of reality, and to make that understanding at least partially conscious.

Agape and *Eros* in Evolution

What is the role of *eros* in Peirce's broad understanding of evolution? In his writings, we do not find an explicit examination of this subject. True, it is implicit in his discussion of *agape* and its contrary sentiments operating in human moral decisions, but for his deeper exploration of *eros* in evolution, we must look to his expositions of semiosis or sign action in the evolutionary process. Here it becomes clear that the work of *agape*, the promotion of the actualization of potentials, is carried out in a rich environment of dynamic signs, and that sign interaction is, more or less, the equivalent of eros-driven love.

Peirce is universally acknowledged as a key player in the establishment of semiotics, the science of signs. His semiotic vision runs throughout his philosophical writings, and its importance for the development of his thought is undeniable. In the discussion of signs that follows, I am indebted to Robert Corrington's lucid examination of Peirce's semiotics.[10]

Peirce defined a sign as something (the sign) that stands in relation *to* something (its interpretant) and *for* something (its object) in some respect or capacity.[11] A sign mediates between its object and its interpretant ("the proper significate outcome of a sign"[12]) and brings them into a certain relation with each other. He intended to define signs in the most general possible way, to convey that everything is a sign to some degree and in some respect, without going so far as to say its being is exhausted in its being a sign.

Here is an example. I notice my friend smiling at me and feel good about that. I was feeling glum, but his smile improves my mood. This is a semiotic moment. My friend (the sign object) gives me a benevolent smile (the sign), which results in me (the interpreter/interpretant) feeling an elevation of mood. My elevated mood is the change in me—the result of the action of the sign (the smile). When I, in turn, engage the next person I meet as a happy person, my happy expression becomes a new sign object, which affects and changes that person, the new interpreter/interpretant. From this example, it is evident that I am involved in a series of signs that, during ordinary interactions, continues to grow and ramify. The richness of semiotic action in the world is well demonstrated by the fact that this event is merely a scrap of what happens to me and the immense web of signs with which I am continually engaged and to which I am contributing.

Peirce tells us "this universe is perfused with signs"[13] and that every existing thing is a sign:

"every picture, diagram, natural cry, pointing finger, wink, knot in one's handkerchief, memory, fancy, concept, indication, token, symptom, letter, numeral, word, sentence, chapter, book, library, and in short whatever, be it in the physical universe, be it in the world of thought."[14]

In the end, Peirce saw the action of signs in the world as universal, not just in communications between people, not just in human contemplation of the world or in the interactions of intelligences that are less than human but everywhere in nature, whether individual intelligences are involved or not.[15] He writes, "Thought [i.e., the development of signs] is not necessarily connected with a brain. It appears in the work of bees, of crystals, and throughout the purely physical world; and one can no more deny that it is really there, than that the colors, the shapes, etc. of objects are really there."[16] In this, Peirce agreed with William James's anti-nominalist stance, contending that relations between things really exist and are not superimposed by the human mind. Robert Corrington comments on Peirce's statement that "the universe is perfused with signs" by noting that sign activity is tied to mentality, so it would make sense to say that nature must be perfused with mentality.[17] In the same way, it might be said that the universe is perfused with meaning. In this connection, it is instructive to consult the following fragment from Peirce's writings:

> The action of a sign generally takes place between two parties, the utterer and the interpreter. They need not be persons; for a chameleon and many kinds of insects and even plants make their livings by uttering signs, and lying signs, at that . . .. However, every sign certainly conveys something in the general nature of thought, if not from a mind, yet from some repository of ideas or significant forms, and if not to a person, yet to something capable of somehow "catching on" . . . that is [,] of receiving not merely a physical nor even merely a psychical dose of energy, but a significant meaning.[18]

Felicia Kruse points out that the triadic relationship of signs is the relationship that underlies the evolutionary process at work in the universe. She also notes that, according to Peirce's "objective idealism," the universe is *mind*, and this applies to "not merely the sensory and cognitive capacities of organisms, but also, and more fundamentally, the intelligibility that pervades the entire universe and serves as the telos of cosmic evolution." Kruse ties this sign action to "Peirce's principle of *agape*, which is the condition for the evolution of new intelligibilities in cosmic evolution"[19]

When we have the experience of being agents of evolutionary love, when we love agapically, we do so through participation in a cosmic force. *Agape* does not belong to us; we do not generate it from within. Rather, we are its channel. *Agape* is embedded in us, as it is in all existent things, but in our case, we also become conscious of it, feel it as a subjective disposition, and decide the degree to which we want to act on it in our dealings with others. *Agape* is an enabling condition or presence that must be in place to make something possible. In this sense, it is a timeless foundational support of our world.

If *agape* is the underlying principle that makes sign action possible, *eros* serves as the means by which that action occurs in the manifest world. Corrington's understanding of the relationship between semiosis and evolution is particularly rich, and, in what follows, I rely heavily on his vision of sign action in nature.

Corrington's philosophy belongs to the general category of "naturalism." Philosophical naturalism comprises several schools that hold that nature is all there is and that there is no justification for believing anything exists beyond or outside of nature. It follows from this that all philosophical explanations of reality must be sought within nature itself. Corrington's form of naturalism, "ecstatic naturalism," posits one nature with two aspects: *nature naturing*, which is the locus of the unfathomable and inexhaustible potencies from which the world we see around us is produced, and *nature natured*, which is the world of existing things, in which semiosis is always and everywhere at work. Since all philosophical explanations of reality must be sought within nature itself, Corrington tells us that the divine must be in and of nature, and he holds that there is a cleft between nature naturing and nature natured, a region that harbors several kinds of "betweenness" or enabling conditions that make the production of our semiotic world possible.

Nature naturing is pre-semiotic. Nature natured is thoroughly semiotic. Nature natured is a realm of signs hungry for opportunity. Here sign action spawns an ever-expanding fecundity of meaning and signification. After describing nature's "hunger" for manifestation, Corrington writes, "At the same time, signs experience their own form of hunger . . .. [A sign] hungers for greater articulation and expression within the realm of semiosis. Signs seek to participate in infinite series in which their own value and meaning is augmented and given novel traits.[20]

Sitting and looking around in my office, I am deluged by a multitude of demanding signs. I have only to look at the cover of one of the books I have written to be affected by a multitude of signs conveying meanings having to do with its writing, its content, its place on the shelf, the personal history of ideas that it presents, and so forth. Insofar as these signs register in my consciousness, each one changes me in an incalculable way, and I become a somewhat different person, altered and moved a little forward on my evolutionary path and ready to become a new sign for those interpreters, now and in the future, who, in their turn, are and will be affected by my changed self. My printer presents me with signs involving my history with that machine, feelings of frustration, gratitude, and continuing wonder at how it can churn out its remarkable products, and these signs have their own ramifying effects on my being. The same can be said about my noisy air conditioner, my faithful microwave oven, the sound of my iPhone ringing too loudly to my left, and so forth. This is to register but a few of the most obvious and most identifiable instances of a flood of meanings that can be made conscious and to say nothing of the input of the much more complex signs generated in my unconscious psyche, reaching me through channels, interior and exterior, that I so little understand. My world is indeed a world with a profusion of signs, vital, pulsating, insistent, and unimaginably effective in the resulting alteration in my being.

In my view, the realm of semiosis is also the realm of *eros*. *Eros* has its own restless hunger, in which the lover desires the love object to be enriched by engaging with it. While *agape* is the universal driver of evolution, *eros* is how evolution occurs on the level of the concrete: of moment-to-moment, day-to-day detail. It is a down-to-earth love in which, by engagement with the love object, the lover reaches out and incorporates some means of growth from that object. All growth, all evolution, happens this way.

As we have seen, *eros* is eager to be enriched through encounters with love objects. It passionately desires or "hungers" to engage with enriching love objects, wherever it finds them. Like sign action, *eros* finds only momentary satisfaction and involves three elements: the lover, the love object, and the relation that occurs between them. *Eros* seeks the satisfaction of the lover. As soon as the *eros*-driven engagement with the love object is over, it is ready to move on to new possibilities of further enrichment. However, the fullest possible satisfaction, the completeness in which the lover can rest and enjoy its fullness, is desired but can never be attained.

The structure of the *eros*-encounter is sign structure, by which the love object (the semiotic object) is encountered through some signified aspect of itself (the sign), by the lover (the semiotic interpreter/interpretant). The result is an enrichment of the lover in which the lover is changed and evolves. The enriched lover is the interpretant (the interpreter of the sign, now changed by the encounter). Using my earlier semiotic example of my encounter with my smiling friend, the love object is my friend, my source of enrichment is his smile, and the enrichment is my elevated mood. This dynamic is happening everywhere, all the time, and, like the action of semiosis in the world, is tireless, unstoppable, and, like the action of semiosis, seeks to involve itself in a ramifying series of occasions of growth.

The sign exchange is an *eros*-driven engagement, where we see evolution happening before our eyes. The love's *eros*-driven desire is a hunger for this kind of engagement, and it finds opportunity to satisfy this hunger at every turn. Objects of *eros* cannot help being sign objects, *eros*-driven lovers cannot help becoming interpretants, and the aspect of the love object that makes itself available and affects the lover cannot help being a sign. In this sense, the universe is both a profusion of signs and a profusion of *eros*. The lover-interpretant, once changed, moves on to the next opportunity, the next object to take in and interact with, the next occasion of evolutionary growth. The hunger of one moment is satiated by the encounter of lover and love object, but then the altered lover moves on, restlessly, to the next moment. In this schema, the love object is desired and affects and changes the lover, but it is not depleted. It remains a rich, full-bodied reality, rooted in the mysterious depths of nature and, in that way, inexhaustible.

In the human (as opposed to the cosmic) form of *eros*-informed interaction, moral choices are constantly being made that involve taking action. The action determines the next love object of the *eros*-desire. The human *eros*-driven agent, by his or her choices, decides what love object (or moment of the current love object) to engage with next. In this decision, it is possible that the action chosen in regard to the new love object will not be sufficiently informed by *agape* and will produce an outcome that is detrimental, or even destructive, for the love object. What happens in the *eros*-informed encounter, as in semiotic interaction, is neither moral nor immoral. The morality is in the choice. Human beings can foresee the outcomes of their decisions. The choice-making is the moral aspect of the encounter, and because the choice is free, it may turn out to be a decision to do something that pushes *agape* out of its proper place of primacy. Then the choice is made without agapic influence. It is *eros* out of touch with *agape*, which is its conscience.

Sitting on the edge of a gorgeous lake in Minnesota, vibrant and unspoiled, I drink in the beauty, and my soul is enriched and elevated through the *eros*-informed encounter. Then my imagination is activated, and I dream of the possibility of many people enjoying similar moments and how that might be made possible by building a condominium on that very shore, which, because of the setting's immense natural beauty, would be attractive for investors, who might make me rich. But I realize that if I turn that dream into a reality, I will have to make decisions for specific actions, decisions that will have momentous implications for that natural environment and initiate processes that could very well destroy that beauty. Here *agape* must come into the picture. Any financial gain I might enjoy could, I now see, be at the expense of the great wonders of nature continuing on their evolutionary path of yet more abundant expressions of beauty. To decide on an action of that kind would be to allow my *eros*-driven pleasures to push aside my agapic benevolence. The dream would be converted into a concrete reality arising from what, on reflection, I might consider a reprehensible moral decision.

All moral decisions, arising as they do from the *eros*-informed encounter, are attributable to the "I," the cause of future events. Sign action has no morality attached to it. Neither does the *eros*-driven exchange. These exchanges are features of nature and simply take place according to the structure of the semiotic world. The moral dimension is added when one decides which action to bring into play and what factors will be given precedence. That decision is the source of the resulting action. The decider, the agent, the cause of future events, is the "I." I am responsible for the foreseeable consequences of that choice. When we talk about moral choice, we refer to choices that take place within reach of our reflective awareness—choices subject to attention and control. In this we are up against the mystery of the "I," that essential part of us that is the seat of decisions, the agent. If it makes real decisions, it does so for reasons. Those reasons may include the given circumstances of the momentary setting, the available objects, the person's unconscious inherited propensities, his or her current understanding of the basis for moral decisions, and so forth. Yet those reasons cannot be totally compelling. If they were, they would not be decisions, only acts compelled by necessity and already determined. Neither can the "I" act from pure blind will, with no reasons. Life experience forces us to admit that although we can and do act freely, we do so for reasons. Not that we are always aware of our reasons. We may imagine we are making a conscious, free decision in a certain situation but then discover there were hidden reasons for the action, silently at work in the realm of the unconscious mind, influencing us in the final choice. So, the "I" freely chooses for reasons, conscious or unconscious, and is the locus of responsibility of our moral decisions.

In human life, this is the structure of our evolution. Once the decision is made, the lover is changed. This is the work of *eros*, altering the lover's "me" and moving the lover forward toward greater fulfillment. Once changed by the sign encounter, the lover-interpretant can also become an object for some new lover, who, in turn, will be changed. In this process, *eros*/semiosis becomes an infinite ramification that continually renews and enriches the world. As Corrington puts it, "the interpretant is always underway toward further interpretants and seems to 'hunger' to link up with larger and larger units of meaning."[21]

Balance of the Two Loves

Iris Murdoch brilliantly describes a moment of moral decision that illustrates how *agape* and *eros* can be combined in a way that benefits both lover and loved one. In her novel, *The Philosopher's Pupil*, she describes the situation of twenty-year-old Tom, who has recently made the acquaintance of Emmanuel "Emma" Scarlett-Taylor, a young man two years his senior. The two are walking along the Thames at night when Tom spontaneously breaks into song, rendering a traditional English ballad in his fine baritone voice. Scarlett-Taylor joins in with a tenor harmony that surprises Tom. He is stunned by the exceptional beauty of his companion's voice. Murdoch describes the situation with her usual psychological acuity:

> When we suddenly learn that some unobtrusive fellow is a
> chess champion or a great tennis player, the man is physi-
> cally transformed for us. So it was with Tom. In the instant,

Scarlett-Taylor was a different being. And in the instant too, deep in his mind, Tom made an important and necessary decision. He was interested enough in singing to recognize an exceptional voice and to covet it. There was a quick tiny fierce impulse of pure envy, a sense of passionate rivalry for the world. But almost in the same moment of recognition, making one of those moves of genuine sympathy by which we defend our egoism, Tom embraced his rival and drew him in to himself, making that superb voice his own possession. He would be endlessly proud of Scarlett-Taylor and take what he later called "Emma's secret weapon" as a credit to himself. Ownership would preclude envy; this remarkable sound and its owner were now his. Thus Tom easily enlarged his ego or (according to one's point of view) broke its barriers so as to unite himself with another in joint proprietorship of the world: a movement of salvation which for him was easy, for others . . . very hard.[22]

Tom had a decision to make: let *eros* dominate and spoil his growing friendship with pangs of envy, or let agapic love have its primacy of place to allow both lover and loved one to grow and prosper. It is important that Tom realizes he has a decision to make, that he could go in either direction and that he and he alone determines the outcome.

Human actions, consciously considered and freely chosen, are the heart of the moral life. Embracing the primacy of *agape* over *eros* is a test of moral courage. We all have moments of weakness, when, in the face of strong *eros*-driven desire, we knowingly choose an action that does not adequately respect the right of the loved one to develop in the way he or she could and fulfill his or her personal potentials. A decision of this kind must be considered a moral failure. But it is a much greater moral failure, even a perversion, when, in feeding our own *eros*-driven need, we desire to prevent the other person's growth and want to destroy a possibility available to the person affected. This is to practice the opposite of agapic love, a failing that is considerably more difficult to forgive oneself for indulging.

When the principle of the primacy of agapic love is reversed, when *eros* is in the ascendant, greed and hunger for power take over. Unfortunately, this reversal is accepted and even elevated as the ideal in large sectors of today's world.

Sounding the Depth of Love

We must not underestimate the power and richness of love. When we attempt to talk about it, we need to use approaches that are adequate to the task. For that reason, I want to take a moment to look at how we perceive objects of our experience, how we arrive at conclusions about them, and how that affects the practice of love.

One thing we know for certain is that what we believe affects how we act. In fact, belief may be defined as an opinion on which a person is prepared to act. That is why it is so important to explore what we believe about love.

As human beings, we naturally search for foundational explanations concerning all of reality: the fundamental nature of things, the origin of the world, the basic constitution of human beings, the meaning of human existence, and the goals of human interactions.

In searching for answers, we begin with our experience. We have to; it is all that is available. William James says of the infant's encounter with the world, "the baby, assailed by eyes, ears, nose, skin, and entrails at once, feels it all as one great blooming, buzzing confusion."[23] Raw experience comes to us completely undifferentiated. By applying our attention to certain aspects of that experience and ignoring others, we pick out combinations that we isolate as "things" and provide with names. James continues:

> Out of this aboriginal sensible muchness attention carves out objects, which conception then names and identifies forever–in the sky 'constellations,' on the earth 'beach,' 'sea,' 'cliff,' 'bushes,' 'grass.' Out of time we cut 'days' and 'nights,' 'summers' and 'winters.' We say what each part of the sensible continuum is, and all the abstracted whats are concepts. The intellectual life of man consists almost wholly in his substitution of a conceptual order for the practical order in which his experience originally comes.[24]

"Carving out" and naming objects occurs because of our ability to focus our attention. We start doing this from the moment we are born. It becomes second nature to us, and we do not realize we are doing it. Without focusing, without paying attention to something and ignoring the rest, and without individuating objects, we would perceive the world as impenetrable chaos and be unable to live a practical life. As time passes, we come to believe the world is comprised of a cluster of pre-existing objects that we "find" there, like rocks lying in a field, and we lose track of the part we have played in cutting them out of the "sensible muchness" in the first place. In this sense, the objects of our experience are not pre-existing things but the result of definitions we impose. This is not to say there are no "things" with their own unity but to point out the significant role our interest plays in setting up the world we experience and making use of it.

As we, as a species, grow more sophisticated in our searching, we carve out objects of experience that, for practical reasons and to extend our knowledge, we give much closer attention and consider unique areas of investigation. A farmer, for instance, constantly scans the data of his daily experience to better understand how to successfully raise his crops. We all carve out such areas of investigation from the plenum of experience to put ourselves in a better position to discover, in a systematic and methodical fashion, important information about an area of interest. We spend a great deal of energy gathering data from within designated regions, which I call data domains. The data domain of a farmer differs from that of a schoolteacher or a carpenter. Elements of these experiences may overlap, but each agent reads the environment from a different perspective and interprets the data according to different practical concerns. Then each person applies his or her perspective to the data to form explanatory theories that give a useful picture of how to deal with that data domain, including formulating a theory that explains something about a particular area of investigation. Theories arrived at through an examination of a domain of experience are necessarily limited, since they are devised to apply to that limited domain and arise from applying a limited perspective to the presenting facts.

Looking at our experience from a broader perspective, we notice something arbitrary about the domains that we, in this culture and at this moment of history, have made objects of systematic investigation. Things could well have been carved up in a different way, and in fact, the carving and recarving continues as we go along, so the boundaries of our data domains are constantly shifting. This is most obvious in the history of the development of the sciences. In our culture, we have based our investigations on what we call the scientific method. Using this method, we have produced distinct disciplines, such as physics, biology, sociology, astronomy, and geology, each with its own domain data. However, this identification of domains is not enough for us. We want to look more deeply and probe the greater depths of our world. As William James points out, we instinctively seek "[t]he principles of explanation that underlie all things without exception, the elements common to gods and men and animals and stones, the first whence and the last whither, of the whole cosmic procession, the conditions of all knowing, and the most general rules of human action—these furnish the problems commonly deemed philosophic par excellence."[25]

We are philosophers. Whether we recognize it or not, we all take up positions on the ultimate issues as we go through life. On a deep, largely unconscious level, we adopt a stance on these matters. We may not realize it until we find ourselves reacting sharply to someone expressing a view contrary to one we have adopted and are shocked into that self-knowledge. So, whether consciously or unconsciously, we are always asking the big *why*—the ultimate *why*. We feel an instinct to ask why and then ask the why of why. Why does this thing move when I push it? Why do power lines hum? Why am I lonely? Why do I have sympathy for others? Why do I seek the truth? Why do I ask so many questions? We answer these questions with some explanation, a theory that accounts for what we experience. If we take the next step and ask what reality stands behind our theories, we are asking the ultimate *why*, the question of our understanding of the entire cosmos, its origin, and its history.

Throughout our lives of wondering, we hit upon answers to our *why* questions. Some of these answers prove their worth, while others, after a period of reflection, we discard. We naturally find ourselves making judgments about which explanations work and which do not, and from these we form the basis of an implicit, but for us compelling, metaphysical vision of the nature of reality. That vision is a hard-won system of beliefs that have survived our winnowing process—the last beliefs standing. For people with inquiring minds, it is natural to keep on asking why to the very end; their beliefs continue to evolve as long as they are alive. This is not to say our ongoing questioning is comfortable. To be a philosopher, and by this I mean a person who makes a point of asking fundamental questions, brings discomfort. It necessarily involves the insecurity of having to constantly re-examine the answers so far attained.

The person who cannot stand such insecurity, who values tranquility of mind above every other consideration, who refuses to surrender cherished convictions in the face of new information, who maintains, at all costs, the safety and comfort of preserving and protecting petrified beliefs—that person, as Peirce says, "blocks the way of inquiry"[26] and betrays both science and philosophy. Such persons shun and fear the great project of humankind to work collectively toward the truth, and their refusal may severely hamper the inquiries of others. To be true to this task, we must not be reluctant to face every reality we encounter. What James called the "stubborn facts" will not give way no matter how uncomfortable they make us feel, and the result of the failure to face them is collective inertia, phobias about the new, and dread of change. This attitude tends to dominate in the worlds of science, religion, education, and politics today, and the effects of this state of affairs on human interactions are devastating. For as I mentioned at the beginning of this discussion of looking deeper into things, if there is one thing we can count on, it is that our beliefs affect our moral choices. Our beliefs about love are central to our personal and social moral lives, and if we hope to make the world a place where love thrives, we must strive to continually re-energize our search for truth, both individually and collectively. So, now I would like to look at the attitude of inquiry we need to adopt to have some hope of success.

The first thing is to be aware of how easily we can jump to conclusions about what we are experiencing. We tend to want to securely formulate our explanations about our experiences as soon as possible, so we can have that matter settled and move on. Unfortunately, this often means being satisfied with pre-judgments—judgments made before all the facts of experience are in. This is where the word "prejudice" comes from, and prejudices of this kind distort our perception of reality and skew our judgments about what are "facts." These prejudices constitute straitjackets to our thinking about what is real and what our perceptions mean.

The principal sources of such prejudgments are: 1) pronouncements from authorities who influence our thinking; 2) unconscious cultural preconceptions arising from the smaller groupings of which we are a part, such as the family, local religious groups, or ethnic communities; and 3) the larger culture, which surrounds us from birth. Cultural forces inculcate standards for living: values, rules about conducting relationships with others, rules about what is acceptable and unacceptable when abroad in society, rituals, fashions, fads, and so forth. We are further influenced by personal encounters, group experiences, and particularly by the various print and electronic media that have come to form the fabric of everyday life. These prejudices can be particularly pernicious when they operate out of sight, in socially isolated or reclusive places where dark innuendo, rumor, and gossip thrive. The difficulty in becoming aware of how cultural beliefs operate in our lives is magnified when they are so broadly accepted, so taken for granted, that our ability to critically identify them is impeded.

The human mind is a marvelous thing. It gives us access to an experience of reality that is astonishing. We can feel reality and move toward understanding it. However, our ability to understand is tied closely to our ability to think abstractly, focusing on just one aspect of reality while putting aside the rest. This is how we formulate abstractions and productively apply them. The ability to form abstractions has given us great gifts, not the least of which is science, with all its attendant benefits. But it can also pull us away from our immediate feelings about reality in its richness, removing us from that primary perspective to such an extent that we lose sight of the inexhaustible profundity of the world and people.

William James expressed this powerfully when he wrote:

> Hence the unsatisfactoriness of all our speculations. On the one hand, so far as they retain any multiplicity in their terms, they fail to get us out of the empirical sand-heap world; on the other, so far as they eliminate multiplicity the practical man despises their empty barrenness. The most they can say is that the elements of the world are such and such, and that each is identical with itself wherever found; but the question Where is it found? the practical man is left to answer by

his own wit. Which, of all the essences, shall here and now be held the essence of this concrete thing, the fundamental philosophy never attempts to decide. We are thus led to the conclusion that the simple classification of things is, on the one hand, the best possible theoretic philosophy, but is, on the other, a most miserable and inadequate substitute for the fullness of the truth. It is a monstrous abridgment of life, which, like all abridgments is got by the absolute loss and casting out of real matter. This is why so few human beings truly care for philosophy . . .. The entire man, who feels all needs by turns, will take nothing as an equivalent for life but the fullness of living itself . . .. he will never carry the philosophic yoke upon his shoulders, and when tired of the grey monotony of her problems and insipid spaciousness of her results, will always escape gleefully into the teeming and dramatic richness of the concrete world.[27]

If we are to understand love, the richest and deepest of our experiences, we must be aware that love, like any other reality, can be examined analytically and reduced to abstractions. But to lose touch with the richness of love would be a great misfortune. So, I want to look closer at how to avoid that. We must be vigilant about the hidden prejudices in our perception of and judgments about reality. For in every case, they amount to abstractions that have removed, blocked out, or distorted "real matter," as James says. When they operate in us excessively, we are the ones who suffer from this de-realizing of reality, this de-naturing of nature.

Solutions Adequate to the Facts of Experience

One view of reality prevails in our broader culture today. It says everything is physical to the core, and all explanations of reality simply involve determining the complex physical mechanisms that nature has evolved to create the world we see around us and to produce our experiences within it. This position has been variously called determinism, materialism, and physicalism.

It derives from that great and powerful abstraction we developed some centuries ago called "science." This view, in modern times, became intimately tied in with Newtonian physics. More recently, deep cracks and gaping holes in this view of reality have appeared and have been increasingly remarked upon. Newtonian assumptions have been the subject of serious criticism from several of the more exacting phenomenologies of our time, from some recent critical philosophical schools and now from science itself in the form of quantum mechanics, which has, in a breathtakingly rapid move, replaced conventional physics. Philosopher Thomas Nagel, who holds a position on this matter reminiscent of Peirce, points out that a reductionist, materialist explanation of our world is simply inadequate. He maintains that a very different way of seeing things is needed, writing that "a genuine alternative to the reductionist program would require an account of how mind and everything that goes with it is inherent in the universe."[28]

Physicalism in its uncritical form is a prejudice, for it automatically excludes certain types of experience based on a preconceived, unacknowledged, and unconsciously protected notion of what is and what is not possible. These are experiences that do not easily fit into a conventional, orthodox view of the world. Yet these experiences occur. For our purposes, we can call them "rogue" facts.

Rogue facts include experiences that are commonly called paranormal or mystical. The book *Irreducible Mind,* to which I contributed, endeavors to take an inventory of such phenomena and thoroughly examine the empirical evidence for their existence. It makes a strong case that such experiences genuinely occur. It further asserts that any complete empiricism must include these experiences, and any theory of reality must take them into account. If we are to clear the way to the deepest possible understanding of love, we must do it based on such a complete empiricism.

The next step is to decide what kind of explanation or theory of reality can adequately account for the facts of such an empiricism. That is what the companion volume to *Irreducible Mind,* titled *Beyond Physicalism,* hopes to accomplish. Discussing the historical point we have reached in our attempts to provide such a broad explanation, *Beyond Physicalism* makes the point that a deterministic materialism or physicalism is inadequate, since it fails to explain how we can have *subjective experience,* much less how the rogue phenomena described above can exist. In the introduction to the book, Ed Kelly points out that most contemporary psychologists, neuroscientists, and philosophers of mind, as well as scientists in general, subscribe, explicitly or implicitly, to some version of ontological physicalism. This view conflicts sharply with traditional and common-sense notions. It asserts that all we are and do can be explained in terms of local interactions among self-existent bits of matter moving in accordance with mathematical laws under the influence of fields of force: "All aspects of mind and consciousness are generated by, or supervenient upon, or in some mysterious way identical with, neurophysiological processes occurring in the brain . . ... Mental causation, free will, and the self are mere illusions."[29] Kelly cites a rising chorus of theoretical dissatisfaction with physicalism as a philosophical position, though he insists that any credible position must remain anchored in empirical science. The intention of this position is "not to *overthrow* science but to *expand* it to dimensions more fully commensurate with the complexity of our subject matter."[30] He discusses this in terms of the "current science-religion debate" in the United States.

> *Most fundamentally, our view is that both sides are mistaken in thinking that they represent the only possible alternatives.* What we are attempting to do here is to open up a third way—a tertium quid—that somehow combines an expanded science with the recognition of genuine empirical realities underlying traditional forms of religion . . .. Our goal is to find or construct a conceptual framework potentially capable of accommodating psi phenomena . . . mystical experiences, and all of the other "rogue phenomena documented in *IM*, as well as phenomena of more everyday sorts, and we are pursuing that goal by bringing together the diverse and normally non-interactive perspectives of empirical science, metaphysical philosophy, and the great mystical traditions with their broadly similar but far-from-identical views. In effect, we are attempting to drive as far and as quickly as possible toward an empirically justified, theoretically satisfying, and humanly useful "big picture" of how things really are and how we humans fit in.[31]

Only such an ambitious project can provide the foundation for developing a deep understanding of the work of love on the cosmic and the individual level. This approach to probing the nature of reality is intimately dependent on the practice of an uncompromisingly thorough phenomenology.

Phenomenology

The great mistake in our approach to understanding the nature of the world and human experience is what I described above as prejudice or a rush to judgment. Premature formulations based on a vision of reality that has been artificially censored to exclude data that fall outside the personal philosophy of the investigator must lead to dead-end conclusions. Phenomenology (the examination of our direct and raw experience of objects) is an essential philosophical tool to apply to our perceptions to exclude, as far as possible, the prejudgments and hidden distortions that underlie our encounters with reality. Only an uncompromising phenomenology, one that sweeps us clean of unrecognized prejudices, will allow us to reach an adequate understanding of the nature of the reality in which we are immersed.

We experience reality in two stages: first is the perception of something, and then judgments are applied to that perception. The perceptions cannot be wrong, but the judgments can be. The problem is, when we have a perception of something, we apply judgments so quickly that we may or may not know we have made them. The judgments can be consciously identifiable, or they may be largely unconscious. In any case, it requires a particularly disciplined approach to avoid making mistakes in our judgments and winding up with a false idea about the experience. A simple example of a false judgment is having a sense perception of a stick in water. The perception of it is a particular set of impressions of colors, shapes, and so forth. But our judgment about the perception may be that the stick is bent. The part of the stick outside the water seems to be straight, but the part of the stick in the water seems to be bent at an angle. As the perceiver gains more experiences with sticks in water, he or she comes to realize that the stick is not bent, but that the refractive qualities of the water make it look so. The perception, as such, was not wrong, but the judgment about that perception was.

A more complex example involving sense perception is my seeing, at some distance, the back of a person who is walking away from me. I might make the quick judgment that this person is a friend I know well. But when I run and catch up to him, I see I was mistaken. My judgment was mistaken, but not my perception. My perception was of a set of sensations, in this case, mainly visual, of colors, shapes, and movements. That perception was what it was, no more, no less. But on seeing this distant figure, I immediately made some judgments about that perception. I thought I recognized the coloring, the shape, and the style of movement characteristic of my friend. I was mistaken.

An even more complex example would be of a perception that takes place largely on an unconscious level. This kind of perception is what Carl Jung called "intuition." Jung defined intuition as "perception via the unconscious."[32] He says that intuition resembles an ordinary process of perception, but, unlike the conscious activity of the senses and introspection, this perception is unconscious. For him, intuition and sense perception are distinct, even antagonistic to each other. People who are busy with what their eyes and ears may fail to notice the signs and images of intuitive knowing. Jung tells us that intuition is neither sense perception nor intellectual inference, although it may show itself to us in such trappings. Rather, it is the direct unconscious apprehension of a highly complex situation. Intuition comes to us as an automatism, an involuntary event. While we tend to experience the content of conscious thinking and feeling as produced or derived through some rational process, in other words, through conscious effort, the contents of intuition are directly given to us. For Jung, intuition is not contrary to reason but beyond reason, a "miraculous faculty" that is accompanied by a feeling of certainty and conviction.[33]

According to Jung, intuition takes place through mechanisms we know little about, mechanisms that allow us to experience direct insights, independent of the senses or intellect. Like sense perception, intuition yields a true impression of the object of experience. It cannot be wrong; its content is what it is. But by the time that intuitive impression works its way up into conscious awareness, the experiencer will have made all kinds of judgments about it. Some of these judgments may be made unconsciously and some consciously. These judgments necessarily alter or distort the original direct impression that is the intuitive perception. Because unconscious perceptions are so different from sense perceptions, we cannot help but interpret them to make them understandable to conscious awareness. Through these transforming judgments, they become available to rational conceptualization and expressible in language.

Here is an example from my experience as a psychotherapist. Early in my practice, I was working with a woman in whose presence I felt an inexplicable fear. Being a conscientious young therapist, I began to examine myself about this fear. Specifically, I asked myself if this was some sort of "countertransference" on my part—a situation in which a therapist experiences subjective feelings about a client that arise from the therapist's unconscious mind, perhaps indicating an unresolved conflict remaining from the therapist's formative years. These sorts of things happen, so I took the matter to my supervisor to explore the possibilities. Try as we might, we could find nothing of the sort. Still puzzled by the experience, at a subsequent session with this person, I suddenly felt a hunch about what might be going on. Based on that hunch, I asked her: "When you come to see me for a session, how do you feel?" She replied, "Oh, I always feel afraid." When she said this, my fear lifted, and from that time on, I never felt fear in her presence. I believe what was happening was that I had an unconscious but direct intuition of fear and had no way to determine if the feeling was hers or mine. The sudden lifting of the fear occurred when (by another intuition) I identified it as hers. My perception of fear was correct, but my judgment that the fear belonged to me was mistaken. I experienced a feeling of fear and, based on my training as a psychotherapist, assumed I was its source. I made that mistaken judgment in an effort to make sense of the perception.

I would like to draw upon my experience for another example, this one more complex, of the altering of unconscious perceptions into forms that can be understood by the conscious mind. Over my years of therapeutic practice, I have discovered that it is especially useful to note impressions that pop into my awareness spontaneously and without preamble. Sometimes impressions of that sort come as pictures or imagined scenes. In my example, I was in a therapy session with a client in my office, while the client for the next session was seated in my waiting room. As I was finishing the session, I was suddenly aware of a visual scene intruding into my imagination. In it, my next client (now sitting in the waiting room) walked through the door into my office carrying a gun. I was rather shocked by this vision and did not know what it might mean, although I made a note to myself to remember it and think about it later.

The next client came in, sat down, and told me that she had become suicidal and felt desperate. She had never spoken of such feelings before, but as she described them, it became clear she was in a seriously disturbed state. I was wondering how to approach the situation with her when the image I had just experienced returned to my mind. In an instant, its meaning became clear. The gun represented her anger, and my approach to working with her should be to help her uncover her hidden rage, which, because repressed, was being converted into suicidal thoughts. Working along these lines, we were able to dissipate her potentially dangerous feelings.

When intuitions arrive as images or symbols, it may be difficult to realize their importance, because the event or situation they refer to may not yet have happened, or the person they relate to may not be present. Intuitions can arrive at the same time as their object or be delayed. Intuitions can show themselves in dreams or in hypnagogic images (which occur in the process of falling asleep or waking up). It is important to recognize the value of such experiences and maintain an attitude of curiosity even about mental/emotional impressions that seem entirely random, meaningless, or bizarre. It often happens that, given attention, they will reveal their intuitive content.

An intuition can also manifest itself as a thought that seems particularly persistent. It starts and insistently develops, pursuing connections with other thoughts, unfolding itself in unpredictable ways, seeming to have a mind of its own. If these spontaneous mental events are allowed, they often lead to surprisingly useful insights.

Although intuitions sometimes come to us in the form of propositions or words, they more often assume the form of symbolic images. In the example I mentioned above, the gun in the woman's hand was symbolic, not a literal thing. We all have our own idiosyncratic symbols, and it is important to learn their peculiar meanings. We cannot be guided by a general diction-ary of symbols but must pay attention to the unique forms taken by our unconscious productions. We must not throw out these unpredictable perceptions just because a premature judgment says they are meaningless. If we want to spruce up our everyday practice of phenomenology, we can start by not rejecting or dismissing perceptual experiences that do not immediately fit in with our current view of reality and by approaching them in a spirit of curiosity rather than fear or distaste.

It is precisely because we make so many automatic and often unconscious judgments about our perceptions that we need a phenomenological approach, separating (as much as possible) perceptions from judgments and arriving (also to the extent possible) at an understanding of our experiences that are free from distortions deriving from judgments based on preconceptions. We are liable to produce these distortions in the ordinary conduct of daily life, but we may also experience them in our intellectual life. This is particularly important to keep in mind when formulating our scientific and metaphysical explanations of reality.

Regarding love, unacknowledged prejudgments can produce grotesque distortions of our experience. How could a full and adequate sense of its nature and function ever be reached by an approach that is satisfied to say that all reality is simply the result of bits of physical material bumping up against each other in fields of force? In my opinion, physicalism is a failed phenomenology. If one espouses physicalism, then the fact of love, a profound reality experienced by all people in all ages, must be judged unreal and explained as a delusion that we construct about something that has no real substance but is merely matter in motion. In such a mechanistic framework, the ancient vision of love as a principle fundamental to the existence of the universe must be looked at as absurd. If the flawed phenomenology of physicalism is accepted uncritically, then nothing meaningful can be said about love except to describe the process by which the material brain constructs such a delusion.

If we were to adopt this inadequate outlook, we would be utterly helpless to discuss the personal and social ills that plague the world—much less propose actions that might remedy those problems. Instead of pursuing that dead-end approach, it seems more sensible to spend our energies seeking the most stringent of phenomenologies and the most fearless and broadly inclusive ways of dealing with the facts of experience to work out a substantial and pragmatically sound vision of the world. Those who include, in their understanding of their experience, a conviction of deep wholeness that involves a sense of direction and meaning in reality rightly demand something that goes beyond the empty abstractions of physicalism, something more adequate to the facts.[34]

Evolution and Choices

How does the sense of wholeness and meaning discussed above play out in regard to our deliberate engagement in the process of evolution? I evolve, and my choices play a key role in that evolution. My actions are motivated by reasons or purposes. Even though some might doubt there is meaning or purpose in the universe, I know I make choices for reasons that relate to my development and growth. I evolve through the growth of self that occurs as I apply my capacities. I evolve over my entire lifetime, and the alterations that occur during that time are such that I hardly know how I can consider myself the same person from beginning to end. How do I know I am the same, that I have continuity of identity? The changes in my self can be so radical that I may be hard pressed to make out what the continuous elements might be. Even possessing the same memories over the years is not a guarantee of continuity, for memories evolve, fade, and, in some unusual cases, disappear altogether. Yet I retain the conviction that, despite all that, I preserve a fundamental identity throughout.

To undertake this investigation, we must return to the problem of the "I." On the one hand, the nature of my "I" seems simple and self-evident. I say "I" all the time, so I must know what it means. On the other hand, the truth is that the "I"—one's own "I" in particular—remains one of the most elusive realities of our experience.

Peirce approaches the "I" and personal identity in the following way. In his scheme of things, to be a person is to be guided by goals, to make decisions to accomplish purposes. A person must possess the power to act, and Peirce identifies this power with the "I": "The leading part of the meaning which we express by 'I' is the idea of an unrestrained cause of some future events . . . the power of voluntary action."[35] This seems to hit the mark about our actual experience of the "I" in making moral decisions. The "I," which has the power of voluntary action and is the cause of future events, is also responsible for the choices made regarding those actions. When I use the word "I," I refer to some specific and undeniable aspects of my experience, namely, 1) that my experiences are mine; I own them, 2) that my voluntary actions are mine; I freely create them, 3) that I have a unique position in the world and a unique perspective on the world, unlike any other.

When we talk about our conscious participation in our own evolution, we are talking about the functions of the "I." We are talking about moral actions chosen consciously. But we are also talking about choices made on the unconscious level of our psyche. The evidence is overwhelming that we have unconscious personal centers that are capable of not only making decisions but also seeing that these decisions are carried out.[36] This makes the issue of determining the nature of personal responsibility in moral decisions a complex one. When we look to unconscious as well as conscious motivations, we must apply subtle, and in some cases, controversial, analyses of moral intent. We must also, acknowledging that the personal unconscious has multiple levels of depth, admit we are dealing with considerable complexity.

Putting aside for the moment the difficulty involved in examining unconscious input into our moral decisions, I would like to concentrate on consciously chosen moral actions. In this it seems that the mystery of the "I," mentioned above, confronts us at every point. "I" have certain unique perspectives on my experience. "I" take actions based on those perspectives. "I" am responsible for my actions. My "I" does not evolve. It remains unchanged throughout. The part that evolves I call, following William James, my "me," my empirical self, the locus of all those changing attributes that I call mine. "I" do not evolve, but I am responsible for the evolution of my "self," my "me." What drives my "I," so to speak, in carrying out this task? It must be *agape*, the driver of all evolution.

When I find myself in a situation that calls for action, I am compelled to make a concrete decision about what to do. That compulsion is inescapable, in the sense that if I decide to do nothing, that decision is a response. The need to make decisions is an essential element of my nature as a human being. If I am alive and conscious, I cannot escape it. In this compulsion, I feel the embedded urge to move, to grow, to evolve. I feel the push of cosmic *agape*.

My decision is not directionless, however. Its direction is toward self-enrichment and the evolutionary advance of my self, my "me." My growth is in the direction of realization of my potentials, of becoming more and more of what I can be. Here I feel the urge of *eros*.

But do my decisions always involve some degree of *eros*? Do I ever experience a purely "self-less" agapic momentum? Maybe not. But perhaps there are times when the urge to action that I feel involves no discernible motive of self-enrichment, when I "forget myself" and act for the benefit of the other alone, when the feeling is simply to further the development of that other. In such a case, there is no desire to build up my personal self, and my "I" becomes an intentional agent of world evolution, an agent of cosmic *agape*.

Love of Oneself

Human beings are in a unique position relative to the universal force of *agape*. As creatures who participate in *agape* as agents of unconditional, benevolent love, we feel the urge to love every existent evolving being. On the other hand, as creatures who are immersed in this world and evolving in it, we experience being loved agapically. So, we can be either an agent of *agape* or its beneficiary. However, as far as we know, we are the only creatures who can love ourselves agapically, who can be both agents of *agape* and recipients of *agape* in one act of love. We find ourselves in two positions simultaneously: the agapic lover and the agapically loved. This is what it means to love oneself.

In the above discussion of the "I" and the "me," I stated that in loving oneself, the "I" loves the "me." My "I" wishes success and fullness of realization for my "me." My "me" is my evolving, growing, changing self that engages the world and people through *eros*, seeking opportunities for enrichment in that engagement. The *eros* operative in my "me" hungers for the fulfillment of my potentials, the realization of my as-yet-unknown possibilities. It is this active self as an expression of *eros*, my "me," that is loved by my "I."

Some spiritual traditions denigrate loving oneself as destructive and immoral. They teach that we must identify only with the agapic force in nature and throw off *eros*. This is impossible, because *eros*-driven activity is essential to the existence and evolution of our world. We must all seek the occasions of growth that will move us forward in the development of our latent capacities. There is no other way. Seen from this perspective, self-love is a virtue, and self-neglect is a failure of agapic love.

Some individuals, perhaps because of their psychodynamic history, find it difficult to love themselves. Peirce has an answer for them in his insistence that agapic love does not require "self-sacrifice."[37] In fact, we must exercise agapic love toward ourselves. We cannot exclude any creature—including ourselves—from that love. This can be a liberating thought for those who are caught in the throes of self-denigration or self-rejection.

Each person is the author of his or her evolutionary advance, which is fueled by *eros*. We have a duty to look after our own growth and fulfillment. As individuals, we and no one else can perform that duty. *Agape* desires our fulfillment and supports us in that endeavor. Rather than viewing our duty to love ourselves as objectionable, *agape* emphasizes its central role in evolutionary growth.

Human Potential and Trance States

Agape is the desire for the greatest possible fulfillment of the loved one's potentials. When it comes to human interactions, loved ones are potentially any and all of the human community. To understand fully the agapic drive for the evolution of humanity, it is important to have a grasp of how human potentials are evoked and actualized.

Human beings are apparently unique in their capacity to contribute to the actualization of their own potentials through conscious choices. This intelligent involvement in our own evolution is something that occurs in large and small ways. Whether the actualizing choices are major or minor, they are woven into the texture of our daily lives. From the first glimmers of conscious deliberation in early childhood to the end of life, we engage with the world in which we are immersed. This engagement evokes our embedded potentials in significant ways and moves us along our evolutionary path.

What I have just said is true enough, but in a way, it might convey an overly individualistic view of our human reality. We do not actually exist as isolatable individuals. It probably would be truer to say that, from beginning to end, we are constituted by and grow through our interactions with each other. These interactions are not just through words and gestures. They are the constant interchanges that happen between us, because we are in the same place, the same group, the same culture, and the same world. We are constantly being recreated by interrelations that are too complex to fully comprehend. We might well say these interactions are the place where we most powerfully and importantly carry on our communication. This may be difficult to see, because we tend to think our communications take place mostly through consciously intended, or at least recognized, encounters with each other. In fact, these types of interactions represent but a speck of our true interconnectedness.

So, when we speak of ourselves as "individuals," it might be wise to put quotation marks around that expression, indicating it is a useful fiction. Like it or not, we are all in this thing together. We can either recognize this fact and make use of the insights that derive from such a recognition or pretend it is not so and be hamstrung by that pretense. This is why the importance of communities keeps coming forward as we explore evolutionary love. We are not individuals who must make strenuous efforts to create communities (although there is, of course, a sense in which that is true); rather, we already live and move and have our being in communities. The more we acknowledge that fact and learn the ways to build truly love-informed communities, the better position we are in to promote the practice of *agape* in that greatest of communities we call the human race.

Granted all this, we still need to talk about ourselves "as individuals," as persons who are responsible for our actions and who have the power to influence, for good or ill, others who are within range of our activity. We "individuals" are intelligent nodes in the larger network of interconnections in which we exist. In other words, we need to be able to talk about our moral lives as decision makers.

Our moral engagement with the world begins with our conscious and unconscious perceptions of our environment and the beings that constitute it. It culminates with deliberate actions, each of which leaves our mark on the world and moves us toward the next moment in our evolution. If we recognize the truth of our deeply founded interconnections, we realize we must engage with the world, moment to moment, whether we like it or not. To make such choices, we must be aware of what is around us and realize that we can reach out and engage with it. This involves focusing on the things we encounter. Focusing our attention on something and deciding how we want to engage it activates our capacity for conscious self-creation. It creates an opportunity to tap our unique, personal fund of potentials. To be fully human is to work constantly at this kind of intelligent self-actualization.

Our evolution through encounters with the world is predicated on our ability to perceive the world in which we are immersed and to focus on its inhabitants. We are constantly shifting our attention from one thing to another. When we encounter something that interests us (for whatever reason), we pay attention to it, focus on it. This is the first step in bringing about self-actualization. If we focus at all, we automatically reduce our awareness of other things and relegate them to the fringes of conscious attention, so our awareness of them diminishes. The more intensely we focus, the less we pay attention to things that are irrelevant to the object of our focus. This state of heightened awareness of the object of our focus and diminished awareness of everything else makes it possible for us to engage effectively with that object. Engagement automatically evokes a response to the object. We are constructed in such a way that, when we engage consciously, we cannot help but mobilize our entire psyche to interact with or affect the object of focus.

Each of us determines what that focus will be. One fine spring day, as I walk from my office to have lunch at a favorite restaurant, a distance of several blocks, I am struck by the sheer beauty of the natural world around me coming to life. I engage with this and then that feature of the awakening environment and am pleasantly stirred by what I see. Overall, my focus is on the wonders presenting themselves. The next day, the scene is the same, another fine spring day, but as I walk, I find myself thinking about a chapter for a book I am writing, and I become deeply involved in trying to solve the problem of how I want to express a certain idea. Now my walk to the restaurant is a very different experience. I am barely aware of the beauty around me. My focus is on the world of my ideas and speculations. Instead of the pleasure of being immersed in a lovely world, I am focused on a series of thoughts that move along a very different path. The glorious surrounding scene, for all practical purposes, disappears. I have made a choice that radically alters my intention and creates a novel combination of ideas for my book, creating a new, unique moment of evolutionary advance.

As I have mentioned, even as we focus consciously on one object, we simultaneously interact powerfully with whatever is within our emotional vicinity. In this state of focus, we draw from a rich fund of subliminal resources, including yet-to-be actualized potentials or capacities, and it can happen that the engagement calls upon some potential in us that has never been manifested. We experience something about ourselves that is truly new. This is how we bring novelty into the world, how we consciously accomplish our evolutionary advance. This is conscious self-creation.

The mechanism that brings about conscious self-creation—focus on some object, diminished awareness of everything else, with the activation of the faculties needed to engage with the object of focus—is the definition of what I mean by a trance state.[38] Trance is the mechanism by which, through deliberate action, we bring about the actualization of our potentials. I will say more about this in a moment, but first I would like to take a brief look at a cultural movement that was heavily engaged with exploring effective ways to promote such actualization.

The Human Potential Movement[39]

The 1960s in the United States saw the rise of a vision of human development that came to be called the "human potential movement." The name was the creation of Michael Murphy and his co-worker, George Leonard, at the Esalen Institute in Big Sur, California. The reality to which it referred was a growing cultural momentum of experimentation with human development on physical, emotional, and spiritual levels. The inspiration for the term "human potential movement" came from Aldous Huxley's expression "human potentialities," which was meant to suggest that human consciousness and human physiology possess untapped and unimagined resources and that techniques to liberate them are within reach. Esalen became a center for the development of such techniques.

The message of the movement was that such techniques, both ancient and modern, could be put into practice by anyone willing to spend the time and effort. The goal was the attainment of a heightened consciousness and a vital and satisfying embodied life. The source of this enhanced consciousness and vitality was identified as a universal cosmic energy. The potential to be actualized by these techniques were, in some cases, manifested in extraordinary and dramatic form, such as paranormal and mystical experiences, and in other cases involved gradual growth. This burgeoning interest in human potentials occurred, in part, because of the availability of new techniques or "technologies" for entering trance states (at the time commonly called "altered states of consciousness"). These included meditation and the practice of yoga, ingestion of psychedelic substances, holotropic breath work, and other body-based healing techniques, as well as the performance of rhythmic activities, such as dancing and drumming. These newly available techniques, whether ancient or recently devised, were powerful methods for creating the desired altered states for releasing human potentials.

Two conditions are necessary for any human potential movement to arise: 1) a belief that all people have unrealized potentials and (2) a technology by which these potentials can be actualized. The first condition is an acceptance that great deeds of human self-discovery are not reserved for a few adepts, and that both the extraordinary phenomena that some people experience and the more everyday kinds of human growth and self-betterment are, in principle, available to all. The second factor is access to a technology that can actualize these potentials at will, for if the rich store of human potentials is to be evoked, experimented with, and put into practice, we must be able to tap it consistently.

Trance States and the Evocation of Human Potentials[40]

When I was examining the practices that grew out of the human potential movement, I could not help but notice that they all involved some form of trance induction. In my studies of the history of trance states, somnambulism, and hypnosis,[41] I found it necessary to work out a definition of trance that would apply to every one of its many varieties. Eventually, I arrived at the following definition: a state of focus on something, accompanied by a diminished awareness of everything else, that evokes subliminal resources appropriate to engagement with the object of focus.

You notice something. If it grabs your attention, you stay with it, at least for a moment. If you find that it interests you, you become engaged with it—it becomes the explicit object of your focus. In fact, people cannot accomplish anything without engaging with an object of focus. For example, an actor becomes absorbed in a role. She may find that her engagement with the role is so profound that she temporarily becomes the person portrayed. On the other hand, we have many everyday examples of trance focus, such as threading a needle (an operation that involves temporary but intense absorption), crossing a busy street, having a deep conversation, giving a speech, making love, and—something we do every night—dreaming.

All conscious human experience is characterized by focus. To be focused on something is to be engaged with it. The engagement may be drawn out over a long period of time, or it may be very short, occurring in the twinkling of an eye. It is the engagement itself, not the length of time it takes, that defines focus. I concluded that if all conscious human experience is characterized by focus, it is characterized by trance.

The effectiveness of the state of focus is determined by its intensity. The greater the interactive intensity created, the more powerful the trance will be for activating unrealized potentials. This is accomplished by finding a way to direct as much energy as possible to the object of focus and to withdraw it from other potential objects, whether conscious or unconscious. Intensity is the determinant of the depth of the trance.

Diminished Awareness

The best index of the degree of intensity is probably the degree of diminished awareness of things outside of the object of focus. When a person focuses on something, everything else is pushed to the fringe of awareness. Although a vague awareness of other things remains, its effects are weak.

Just what might this focus/fringe experience look like? Let us say I am staying at an old inn on a lake. In the morning, I look at myself in the antique bathroom mirror. I wonder if my beard needs a trim. I examine it closely and decide it does. I turn and reach for my trimmer, and when I look back at my reflection, I see that the mirror has several small spots where the silvering has disappeared—a clear sign of age. I had not noticed the spots on the glass before; all I saw was my face and beard. If I had been called out of the room as I reached for my trimmer and asked whether the mirror was suitable and clear, I would have responded in the affirmative. But now I see the spots and turn my attention to them. Looking closely, I note their position, their shape, their color. I see that they form a peculiar pattern—an arrangement of oddly shaped circles—that interests me. As I focus on the spots and the patterns they form for me, I become increasingly absorbed in them.

For a moment, my focus on the mirror and its defects is so intense that I have almost no awareness of the reflection of my beard and my face. I concentrate on the odd spots and speculate, wondering how old the mirror is, whether this kind of defect occurs in all older mirrors, and what are the chances that this fascinating pattern of spots would eventually repeat itself in a mirror of the same manufacture. In such moments not only do I lose awareness of my beard, I also do not notice the passage of time, and momentarily, I even forget who I am—I am totally absorbed.

Now I realize that I have completely lost awareness of my face, even though I am staring at its reflection. I have also lost awareness of the trimming project I had set for myself. My initial scrutiny of myself in the mirror has shifted to a fascinated examination of the mirror itself. My focus has shifted, and so has the group of sensations that form the fringe of my awareness.

Now I am intrigued by what has just happened. I reflect on the general fact that what I concentrate on at any moment is my focus, and what I am not concentrating on moves to the fringe of my awareness. These internal reflections become yet another center of focus, and now both beard and mirror are pushed to the fringe of my awareness. I can shift at will the focus/fringe structure of my experience. Now beard as focus with the mirror itself as fringe. Then it is the mirror with its spots as focus with my beard as fringe. Finally, my thoughts about focus and fringe take over as the center of attention. With each shift of focus, the previous focus is forced to the periphery of my awareness.

We also spend time in lengthier states of focus. When we go to a movie theatre and become absorbed in what is happening on the screen, we quickly lose awareness of the theatre itself and the people around us. This absorption in the movie and obliviousness to everything else can become so profound that we feel we are there (in the movie) and not here (in the theatre). We may experience an altered sense of time and even lose track of the involvements of our current life. If the movie trance is deep, when we leave the theatre and our awareness broadens, we might feel as though we have been somewhere else and momentarily find the world around us odd or alien.

But we do not need to be sequestered from the world to have such experiences. Some people find that diminished awareness of their surroundings can occur when they read a good book or hear a stirring piece of music. I know one person who becomes so absorbed in music of a certain kind that he loses awareness of his surroundings and focuses totally on the images and feelings the music evokes for him. This state can be so pronounced that, for safety's sake, he can only allow music to take over in this way when he is safe at home.

The degree of diminished awareness is an index of the intensity and depth of a trance. The deepest and most intense trance is a phenomenon in which someone exhibits an unwavering focus and nearly total lack of awareness of anything not in some way part of that focus. Dreaming is a good example of a deep trance state.

Subliminal Resources

We are all the living repositories of vast inner resources that we can bring to bear on our lives at a moment's notice. Such subliminal resources (coming from below the threshold of consciousness) derive from five main sources: our evolutionary inheritance, our overlearned habits (acquired habits or skills that have become automatic), our unconscious mental/emotional world, our direct but unconscious connection to our immediate environment, and our access to what might be called a form of cosmic creativity.

Some combination of these subliminal resources is always evoked in the trance state. When Nijinsky, the renowned Russian ballet star, danced his incredible performances, he did so, by his own description,[42] in a profound state of trance, and as he danced, he became the living embodiment of a vast array of subliminal resources. He was using the collection of overlearned habits that were the hard-won result of long training and practice. This automatism allowed him to become suffused with powerful emotions arising from his unconscious life, emotions that were crucial to his dramatic performance. Despite his well-publicized mental disturbances, this remarkable artist became the vehicle for a transcendent creativity that was, to him and to all who saw him, an opening to a mystery beyond rational description. Focus is the key to opening the creative resources of the subliminal. The more intense and prolonged the focus and the more exposed the subliminally based roots of perception and action become, the more a person will experience the richness of the normally hidden powers of the unconscious mind.

But we do not have to look to individuals of extraordinary talent to find examples of the conscious mind tapping into subliminal resources in trance states. Take the writer at his keyboard. His absorption in his task activates a variety of such resources. There are the overlearned habits that allow him to type without conscious involvement in the specific movements that his fingers perform to find the correct keys. Ideas relevant to his work arise spontaneously from his subliminal consciousness. Unconscious emotional responses to the subject matter may play their part, and, if he is fortunate, so may creative inspirations. Or take the locksmith who experiences a variety of subliminal interventions that blur together in the complex procedure involved in finding a way to open a lock with no key. In fact, nearly all our daily tasks involve a focus that evokes just such highly interwoven and complex subliminal responses, yet during daily life, we pay little attention to this fact.

Looking at human life from an expanded evolutionary point of view, we can see that trance states are the mechanisms by which we move forward on our evolutionary paths. Each person has an evolutionary path that leads to his or her fulfillment, a path that entails responding to the things, people, and situations he or she encounters. This is the way our potentials are realized. All these encounters with the world take place in some sort of trance state.

Subliminal resources exist within us in two forms: (1) already actualized, habitual capacities that lie dormant but fully formed and ready to be evoked in response to the trance object, and (2) potential capacities that are actualized for the first time.

Largely habitual capacities that are already actualized make up the stable background against which we live our daily lives. Colin Wilson called this aspect of a person in routine engagement with the world the "robot." Even those who achieve great things operate mainly from previously actualized capacities. Where potentials are being actualized for the first time, individuals push beyond what has already been achieved, beyond the "robot," and move themselves forward in their evolutionary development.

When considering these factors, we should keep in mind that all the processes involved in the actualization of potentials operate under the influence and at the behest of *agape* as evolutionary love. Through *agape*, the drive for actualization of human potentials is made possible. The discoveries of the human potential movement highlight the ways *agape* works among us. Advances in our understanding of trance states and the key role they play in our evolutionary growth increase our awareness of our ability to choose how *agape* manifests through us. The essence of *agape* in regard to human evolution is its power to ensure the development of human potentials. The means for achieving this development is the induction of trance states in which *eros* becomes active. Now I would like to make the ubiquitous manifestations of trance states more explicit.

Four Trances

When I arrived at what I believed to be a workable definition of trance, it became apparent immediately that it applies not just to a few special experiences but to all human engagements with life. In daily life, we focus on whatever interests us at the moment, and that focus brings with it a corresponding degree of diminished awareness of everything else. This is the way we conduct our lives and the way we grow.

It came to me, while I was writing my first formulation of the nature of trance states in 1997,[43] that it would be helpful to divide trances into separate categories, according to the object of focus. As a psychotherapy clinician, I discovered that discussing the characteristics of different kinds of trances with my clients proved tremendously useful for therapeutic work and for a deeper understanding of human interactions in general. I realized that proposing categories for trances would have a certain arbitrariness about it and that another person might devise quite a different set. Nevertheless, it seemed useful to make the attempt. So it was that I came up with four types of trances. The first three seemed obvious enough. The fourth, although not obvious, turned out to be of great importance. Here they are.

A *situational* trance involves immersion in and focus on an activity, project, work, or enterprise to the exclusion of other interests. As a rule, the more engrossed one is in the situation, the better one does. People who are successful with their projects tend to be capable of entering a deep situational trance. Examples of situational trances are typing a letter, threading a needle, watching a play, addressing a staff meeting, performing a dance, and writing a book.

In an *interpersonal* trance, one person is focused on another and oblivious to other matters. This kind of trance is at work in everything from concern for a friend to worry about an intimate partner, from annoyance with a co-worker to loathing for a sadistic abuser, from flirtation to lovemaking, from interest to obsession.

An *inner-mind* trance occurs when attention is withdrawn from the concerns of the external world and focused on images and impressions of the inner mind (the world of thoughts, feelings, images, and other impressions). Dreaming is an inner-mind trance that occurs every night, although we may not always remember we have dreamed. In dreaming, the external world is blotted out, and images of the inner mind dominate. For that reason, dreaming is the most profound inner-mind trance we can have. Other examples of common inner-mind trances include worrying, driving while preoccupied, being "lost in thought," daydreaming, and meditation. I also count hypnosis as a species of inner-mind trance and define it as an inner-mind trance that is accompanied by a rapport or special connection with the trance inducer.[44]

The trance that is least recognized but very significant in our lives is the *group-mind* trance. Here the individual becomes a participant in the values and drives that characterize a group. Group minds operate as social organisms, living things that influence the thinking and actions of their members. As organisms, they have the drive to protect themselves and grow, and as organisms, they subjugate the part to the whole. While immersed in the group mind, people may think and act in ways that are in accord with group thinking but out of character with how they behave when apart from the group. Group-mind trances can occur in connection with such groups as one's family, church, or club; at sports events, rock concerts, tenants' meetings, or political conventions; or when one is involved with colleagues at work or friends at a social gathering. More sinister examples include riots, lynch mobs, and fanatical cults. A group-mind trance, in its broadest form, is a cultural trance, which may be thought of as a group-mind trance on the level of an entire people.

Trances are the mechanisms through which *agape* finds expression in human life. Trances naturally result in actions, and insofar as these actions are chosen consciously, they form the substance of our moral lives. Our concrete moral decisions and how they occur in the ordinary course of human living are the subject of the next chapter.

Chapter 2: Love in Action

Up to this point, I have been writing about evolutionary love or *agape* largely as a philosophical concept. To do justice to it, however, I would like to describe it as a subjective experience.

When we have the experience of being agents of evolutionary love, when we love agapically, we do so through participation in a cosmic force. *Agape* does not belong to us; we do not generate it from within. Rather, we merely channel it. *Agape* is embedded in us, as it is in all existent things, but in our case, we also become conscious of it, feel it as a subjective disposition and decide the degree to which we want to act on it in our dealings with others.

Cosmic *agape* is pre-temporal, an enabling condition. An enabling condition is a state of affairs that that must be in place to make something possible. In this sense, it is a timeless foundational support of our world. When we have the experience of participating in cosmic *agape*, we lose our sense of having a self. We do not have to cultivate or force the sense of selflessness in agapic loving; there is no self. When we love agapically, we love from the position of the divine, from the place where the universe as divine moves its evolutionary transformation forward. Although we are embodied beings, in the experience of *agape,* we lose our sense of location in space and time in a body. We are nowhere in particular, appreciating the world, wanting the best for the world, with no sense of desire and no personal expectations about what we encounter.

As conscious participants in cosmic *agape*, we feel it constantly urging itself into our awareness. Whenever we encounter our co-evolving partners in this world—and that means every existent thing—*agape* moves to the fore, ready to exercise its benevolence through us. True, it may be blocked by various personal complexes that blind us to its urge or make us turn it away because of conflicting desires arising from *eros*, but it is nevertheless a kind of instinct that is ready to reach out, desiring that the object of our attention—the loved person or entity—attain the fullest realization of its potentials.

When participating in cosmic agapic love, the human lover does not love to gain some personal benefit. *Agape* is benevolent and unconditional in us, and although we might experience exercising agapic love as pleasurable and gratifying, such enjoyment is not the motivation for loving. Loving agapically can bring with it a feeling of transcendence, of tapping into a deep and primal reality. It is felt keenly when undergoing a mystical experience. It can create in the lover a unique feeling of being part of the creative rhythms of nature itself.

Agape as Feeling

The actual practice of *agape* is difficult. The great challenge in the practice of agapic love is to believe and to feel that every human person, every living being, and every existing reality is a rich repository of unrealized potentials that deserve to be appreciated and supported. An intellectual acceptance of this attitude is not the same thing as believing and experiencing it. The actual practice of *agape* and arriving at the proper balance between *agape* and *eros* in moral decisions is more difficult where belief and feeling are weak.

Difficulties arise, most troublingly, in situations in which the object of *agape* develops attitudes or carries out actions that, in the judgment of the agapic lover, are morally questionable. However, although *agape* requires love of the person, it does not require agreement with the actions of that person or unquestioning approval of how that person lives. It may be tempting to hold those disapproved actions or attitudes against the person and, on that basis, deny agapic love to the person. But the practice of *agape* does not give us the right to impose our moral standards on the loved one.

Further, *agape* is incompatible with the notion that substantial evil exists. It does not accept that a person can be evil, in the sense of being devoid of potential for good. *Agape* wishes well to everything and everyone. It desires the other person's greatest evolutionary development, but that person alone is morally responsible for what actions he or she takes to achieve that end. No person can be denied *agape* because of the state of his or her moral life. No matter how bad a person may be thought to be, he or she is still a real, living, free creature. To love someone with agapic love does not mean we must like the person, trust the person, or approve of what he or she does. *Agape* is more substantial than merely liking someone or approving of his or her actions. Liking a person is a state based on many personal and emotional factors. Approving someone's actions is another position, based on one's personal moral standards. *Agape*, on the other hand, is a state based on the foundational nature of the universe as an evolving reality, which includes human beings, who have the gift of free choice. We can wish them the best, but we cannot take away their moral responsibility for making the choices that will decide who they become and what they do. Because of this, we may not like many people, and we may disagree with or even abhor their choices, but we cannot, based on our judgments about these things—or any other basis—take away their right to be loved agapically. This is an irreducible and uncompromising characteristic of *agape*. Take it away, and it is no longer *agape*. Take away *agape*, and there is no evolving universe.

Agape says that all potentials are, in themselves, positive values. How those potentials are put into action is another matter, a moral matter. The loved one may indeed do evil things, but *agape* does not require us to approve of such things. *Agape* respects the right of all persons to live their own lives and make their own free choices according to their personal judgment. A corollary is that no one can truly judge the heart of another. One person cannot judge the inmost moral state of another person, and no one can withhold agapic love on the grounds of such a judgment. It is hard to imagine a precept more sharply opposed to what many would imagine to be the legitimate limits of love. There are no limits and can be no limits on *agape*, in the sense that some persons must be denied *agape*. *Agape*, in its very nature, is given without consideration of merit. If *agape* were bestowed based on the deserts of the loved one, it would not be *agape*.

This raises the question: must we love agapically even those who have committed atrocious crimes against their fellow human beings? To this question *agape* must answer with an unequivocal "Yes." By loving them, are we saying we like them or that we condone their actions? Absolutely not. But does it mean we must wish that they eventually become fully evolved persons, despite all evidence to the contrary? Yes. This is the answer *agape* would give. So, it seems, would Jesus, who counseled: love the sinner but not the sin.

One might ask, "Does loving even reprehensible people agapically make them more powerful in their evil actions?" Absolutely not. *Agape* is something we carry and feel in our hearts. It does not support or strengthen the evil actions of the loved person in the theatre of human life, and it does not promote actions that would do so. Quite the contrary, we can and must restrain or punish, by any means that is appropriate, people who commit evil actions, even while we continue to love them with the love of *agape*.

Agape and the "I"; *Eros* and the "Me"

As I have mentioned, the exercise of agapic love in human form is associated with the "I" that loves, that elusive source of awareness and action that is unique to each person and which is at the same time rooted in the mysterious depths of the creative power of nature. I love my daughter. I love this orchard. I love this idea. I love you. Philosophers of all ages have attempted to describe this most intimate and unique aspect of the human being. When we say "I" and then try to reflect and describe what this "I" is, we realize we do not know. Some have approached the mystery of the "I" by saying what it is not, by negating those things that are not essential to our unique, dimensionless, timeless core. But what is left over at the end of the exercise still escapes our grasp. Qualities not attributable to my "I" include such things as my physical characteristics, my temperament, even my thoughts. William James conveniently ascribed those familiar aspects to the "me," the personal self about whom one can make certain statements (e.g., having a specific name, living in a particular location, having a particular hair color, possessing a certain body build, certain personal relationships, certain values, certain ways of taking up a challenge, etc.). These characteristics do not define my ultimate irreducible active core, my "I," the source of my decisions and the agent of my actions. For even if all these qualities were to change, my "I" would persist as my single, unique identity.

Changing or evolving aspects of the self are attributable to my empirical "me," and all that makes up my "me" is associated with *eros*. Through *eros* I grow and evolve, developing those qualities that belong to the "me." This process is such that, over time, it is hard to say that I am the same person. But in fact, I am, and what gives me that unchanging, unique identity is the "I." *Eros* brings about enriching changes in the lover; it seeks opportunities to evolve. As an agent for personal evolution, *eros* relishes growth. For *eros*, care and cultivation of the "me" is uppermost.

Eros needs time to accomplish its tasks. The practice of *eros* involves successive encounters and progressive change. One moment of *eros* leads to the next. Of its very nature, the life of *eros* is thoroughly temporal. But while the action of *eros* is immersed in time, *agape* is not. Rather, it is one of the conditions that make time possible.

While *eros* is associated with the "me" aspect of human beings, the agapic is associated with the "I" aspect. The "I" stands beyond time and provides an unchanging identity that grounds change. This does not mean the "I" is a kind of substance, a featureless substrate beneath the flux of changing qualities. This, too, must be denied of the "I." No matter how we try to approach it, the "I" remains a mystery.

It is possible, however, to sense the mysterious depth of the "I." It is actually possible to speak the word "I" and feel the reverberations of its power. The speaking becomes an evocative work of art. Through it we experience the depth of that nature, from which we take our being. However, this experience is ineffable and indescribable; what it gives is more powerful and more transformative than any concepts or terms we might use to describe it. Because of the intensity of our ongoing engagements, it is hard to hold on to such experiences. Reflection does not help, for reflection itself destroys the experience. Nevertheless, such moments leave lasting effects, even though they are not reducible to intellectual knowledge.

All of this is to say that *agape* operates on an entirely different plane from *eros*. It puts us in direct touch with the full power of nature in a way that *eros* cannot. This is further confirmation that *agape* must be the final guide for moral decisions. When it is excluded from or given little consideration in such decisions, we create moral disasters.

Agape as Practice: What Are the Works of Love?

It is important to investigate love in action. Moral decisions cannot be made based on some practical manual of rules. The flow of the currents of love throughout our lives are such that we can only make informed decisions when we fully recognize our unique position in nature.

The work of *agape* is to support the conditions that allow the love object to realize its potentials. The work of *eros* is to seek out and engage with potential sources of enrichment for the lover. The works of love are carried out through our choices. In much of daily life, we do things out of habit and without creative reflection. Nevertheless, every day we make conscious, deliberate choices. These choices constitute our moral life. In these choices, love is always involved.

Rarely, if ever, is only one of the two loves involved in our choices. Our motivations naturally are a mixture of the two; including elements of benevolence and desire. Perhaps the feeling of love for an infant and the desire for that infant to grow to be whatever it can and find its unique way through life is the closest thing we experience to unalloyed *agape*. Another example is the love for nature that we experience when we encounter it in its innate beauty. Here, too, we can feel a benevolent desire that it continue along its evolutionary way and prosper.

Examples of the experience of unalloyed *eros* are more difficult to talk about. The desire for enrichment and growth through encounter with a love partner, for example, is problematic if it lacks a strong element of *agape*. Where *eros* felt for a partner includes the desire for mutual benefit and the intentional promotion of the partner's growth—in other words, an agapic element—it moves both lover and loved one along their evolutionary paths. If *eros* in a personal relationship lacks any trace of genuine agapic concern, it is immoral, and we hesitate to call it love. Any case in which *eros* is bereft of all agapic accompaniment treads on dangerous ground. *Agape* is the conscience of *eros*. *Eros* unrestrained by *agape* can devour the loved one, desiring to be enriched even to the detriment of the loved one. This is true not only in personal intimate relationships but also in any situation in which desire overcomes benevolence, whether the *eros*-driven lover is exercising a duty of trust, negotiating a business transaction, or engaging in any other activity involving another person or persons. Sooner or later, unrestrained *eros* will end in abuse of the desired love object. This applies equally to situations in which the desired object is the natural environment.

Having a guiding moral principle does not make moral decisions easy. In fact, decisions are not reducible to any simple formula. Life and people are profoundly rooted in the depths of nature, and we are limited in our ability to consider the full multiplicity of elements in any decision. We can only do our best. For this reason, we must be ready to acknowledge that we can make mistakes. No aware person can go through life without regrets.

We rightly feel we are responsible for our deliberate decisions. Each one of us is in charge of our own life. Our choices originate with ourselves and no one else. Each one of us determines our life course as we move from decision to decision. It follows that no person can make life-determining decisions for another person; we cannot interfere in the life path of another or put ourselves in charge of another. To presume to do so is to imagine one can put oneself beyond the timeless structure of nature itself.

Custodial Love

My statement above, that "*Agape* is the conscience of *eros*," means we must not interfere with another person's sovereign choices. To this point, I have been speaking of intrusive interference with the choices of an adult, a person capable of making significant life choices. But we should also consider what one might call custodial love, which plays a crucial role in human development.

Custodial love is exercised in situations in which the loved one is unable to make informed moral decisions or is in some way limited in that regard. Custodial love is most conspicuously present in the relationship of parents and children. Newborn infants cannot make conscious decisions about even the most elemental actions involved in their care. Parents are responsible for deciding what is best, from moment to moment, day to day.

These acts of care are heavily weighted toward the agapic. Parental decisions about custodial love must not be made in terms of the parents' personal comfort. Parents are not there to be enriched by the infant—although, of course, great enrichment does occur through loving their children. Parents' custodial care is aimed at providing the conditions in which infants will prosper. It is aimed at carrying out the work of *agape*.

Parents naturally feel agapic love toward their children in infancy. They wish the best for them and do not demand that their little children do things that will enrich the parents. Good parents create an environment that protects their children and gives them opportunities to grow and find themselves. Agapic love is dominant.

I worked with a woman who recounted frequent childhood experiences of intrusive, smothering demands by adult family members who sought self-gratification from children. In family social events, she suffered great discomfort and humiliation because of the conduct of adult relatives toward both her and her brother (from when she was seven years old and he five). These events were characterized by scenes in which the adults insisted on hugs, kisses, and other types of physical contact that were totally unwanted by the children but treated as entitlements by the adults. She would avoid the living room as much as she could. But when she could not, she would be touched and pawed in various ways, all under the pretense of affection. The children felt no affection for these adults, because they knew with unerring certainty that these adults had no true affection for them. They knew what was really happening was that the adults were taking something for themselves. In those situations, she saw her little brother squirming with discomfort and repulsion as those rituals were carried out. And they were carried out with impunity and the full support of her parents, who would shame their children if they did not want to "kiss Grandma" or sit on Aunt Ida's lap or let Uncle John pat their behinds. There was no awareness on the part of her parents or the other adults about how the children felt. It was unrestrained and depraved *eros*. Agapic love, which should be dominant in the exercise of custodial love, was pushed aside in a shameful exhibition of selfish actions that, incredible as it may seem, purported to be expressions of love. Children are not fooled. They know when they are being subjected to intrusive self-serving impulses coming from adults. On the other hand, they can also identify genuine love and affection from adults and respond with affection in return.

In families in which genuine custodial love is in place, a process important for the development and growth of children occurs. I refer here to the assistance custodial adults provide to help children learn about the practice of agapic love. The potential to love agapically exists in all human beings from birth; it is present as a fundamental instinct. But children are in the process of mental and emotional development and not yet consciously aware of this instinct and how it works. A child's affective world is dominated by *eros*, and that is perfectly natural. Children must first learn to care for their own needs and achieve their own development. This is the task of *eros*. Children are constantly enriching themselves physically, mentally, and emotionally. But along with that growth and development, children gradually learn to recognize the agapic love that moves deep within. This means they become aware of feeling agapic love toward their parents and others. This growth accelerates as children develop a social life with other children. They are taught about unselfish actions and the first buds of the love of friendship show themselves. Children also discover that they love things not just to make them feel good or for what they can get from them but also because they are beautiful and because they exist. They become aware of *agape* in the experience of love for what is lovely, both in others and in their environment.

But the growth of a child's ability to love should also stir a new development in parents: the recognition that the child is a person who has a growing mental and emotional life. Naturally, as time goes on, parents are enriched by the increasingly loving response and appreciation they receive from their children. This is natural, and children and parents profit if the proper balance of *agape* and *eros* is maintained. However, that balance may be shaken under the pressures of life. As the relationship develops, parents need to gradually relinquish their protective grip and lessen their decision-making roles with their children, allowing more and more scope for their children to make their own decisions about how to develop their potentials and, in the process, have the exhilarating experience of progressively discovering who they are. In other words, the exercise of *agape* continues for the parent, accompanied by the recognition that their children are developing toward adulthood and must be allowed to find their own way in life.

Shifting Roles

Many parents have a difficult time backing off and letting their relationships with their children evolve in such a way as to allow them the freedom to individuate. As their children move beyond infancy, the situation gradually alters. Growing children are emerging persons and rapidly develop the ability to make choices for themselves. Individuals are coming into being. As this happens, parents must struggle to keep up with the changing situation. Parents have to be careful to gradually relinquish their custodial role. Custodial love, when it does not evolve properly, can turn into the intrusive exercise of power over children. Working with the interplay between providing responsible care and creating space for children to exercise choice can be difficult, and both parents and children must find their own way.

A crisis in this alteration of roles typically occurs during adolescence. Children/emergent adults usually experience a sudden burst of energy for independence and freedom, and the suddenness of the change and its power can rattle their parents. From their own insecurity, parents can easily make the mistake of clamping down and opposing their children's desire for individuation and self-realization. The path of this evolving relationship between children and parents is neither smooth nor straight. Adolescents feel a powerful urge to move out from under their parents' protective care and find their authentic independent identity, but this sentiment surges and wanes as the process moves forward. One day the desire for freedom and autonomy asserts itself, but the next day, the desire to be looked after returns. Nevertheless, the overall movement is toward self-definition. The art of parenthood is to discover where adolescents are on this path and respond appropriately, with the emerging adults setting the pace.

All parents struggle with the continually changing balance of *eros* and *agape* in their love for their children. They struggle as their children move increasingly into developing those potentials that, when the children were infants, the parents' agapic love anticipated. But life is lived in specifics, and the real-life difficulty of releasing children to their own autonomy may be undermined by a subtle form of selfish concern. Parents may find themselves wanting to influence their children to choose patterns of conduct or personal or professional development that will make the parents feel good or proud. Here the desire for personal enrichment on the part of parents plays too large a role. This may eventually erupt, for example, in parents applying pressure on their children's choices of profession, education, friends, and even spouses, to live vicariously through their children instead of encouraging them to discover who and what they want to become. Some parents do not make the transition gracefully. Their misguided ideas can reach such an intensity that they feel entitled to make their young adult children's decisions for them—at which point *eros* throws off the restraints of *agape* and becomes devouring. It grows deaf to its agapic conscience.

Human beings also exercise custodial love for their broader natural environment. In this area, a responsible lover may have trouble discerning the difference between the exercise of care and the exercise of power. Developing an attitude of responsible care regarding the environment is a matter of great importance. Unfortunately, cultures that are enamored with exploitative greed are unlikely to understand that nature is a living reality that deserves the loving consideration of *agape*, that here, too, *agape* must be given primacy.

Intimate Love

Another example of the difficulty in balancing *agape* and *eros* is found in intimate personal relationships. When the love of desire occurs between persons, it is a relationship that is felt as a mutual connection. It forms an emotional field in which each desires to be connected to the other for all they are and all they have to offer. Each feels love toward the other. A loop of energy exists between the lovers from which each one draws and feeds. Agapic love desires the enrichment of the loved one. In a healthy relationship, *eros* is also present, and both persons desire and are enriched by the other's love. Where the contributions of the two partners are fairly equal, the loving bond continues to strengthen. When they are unequal, it weakens.

In his book, *The End of Sex,* American writer and educator George Leonard's description of the intimate love of a newly married couple presents a marvelous depiction of the powerful energy of the sexual encounter.

Here an intense level of interest in each other is in play. The love of desire creates many levels of connection and inter-stimulation, from the most basic physiologically embedded awareness and response through cultural conditioning and previous personal experiences to the most spiritual aspects of personal interaction. As the couple intermingles sexually, a complex network of psychological and physiologically-based events occur that tighten and strengthen the mutual focus. Much of what occurs is inexpressible in language, and typically little verbal interaction is involved; nevertheless, the intensity of communication is great. As each partner grows more in tune with and responsive to the other, the focus is strengthened. As the intensity of focus increases, awareness of anything unrelated to the lovemaking process diminishes, to the point that a degree of loss of orientation in time and space occurs. Only the most urgent and insistent extraneous sense stimuli can penetrate this mutually created world, and this holds true until the sexual act is complete.[45]

An intimate relationship is shot through with mutually active *eros*. Each partner desires to be close to the other, to be seen and appreciated by the other, to be emotionally and sexually nourished by the other, and to be protected and supported by the other. These sentiments enhance both lovers and contribute to their evolution and growth. Each partner also desires the fulfillment of the other, the fullest possible actualization of the partner's potentials. Here *eros* and *agape* are balanced.

Because of the complexity of elements that must be considered, this balance is not easily attained. Iris Murdoch, describing the thoughts of one of her characters who is struggling to love well, writes: "Most of our love is shabby stuff . . . but there is always a thin line of gold, the bit of pure love on which all the rest depends—and which redeems all the rest."[46] That thin golden line of agapic love is what redeems all intimate love. But how is this to be achieved in practice? What happens when, for example, the developmental fulfillment of Partner A meets a curtailment of physical and emotional benefits because Partner B, in striving for her own fulfillment, denies some sexual pleasure or some support to Partner A? In looking after her own growth and development, Partner B may feel she must carve out space, a kind of elbow room, that allows her to expand and become herself. But this necessarily affects Partner A. As happens sometimes, Partner A may find this an impediment to his full physical and emotional expression and the fulfillment of his desires regarding Partner B. The task that stands before this couple is to discover if some accommodation can be made that leaves the intimate relationship intact. In this accommodation, if it is to be successful, each must promote the developmental needs of the other and still allow personal *eros* to flourish.

In the midst of such a conflict, the couple may look for therapeutic assistance. If the psychotherapeutic discussions are dominated by the individuals' separate sexual and emotional desires, the attempt will probably fail. On the other hand, if there is sufficient agapic love, cherishing love, on the part of both partners, success is possible. However, if *eros* floods these discussions, whatever agapic love exists may well be drowned out. If the couple cannot give primacy to agapic love, if, in the turmoil of unsatisfied personal needs, they lose touch with the agapic love element, there can be no satisfying intimate relationship. If both partners allow agapic love its primacy, they will be able to listen to each other, and, it may be hoped, learn to understand each other and discover ways to make the relationship work.[47]

This is why, in a relationship in which one or both partners have a large dose of narcissism, the process aimed at resolution will be constantly thwarted, for narcissism is a condition in which *eros* usurps a place of primacy, and self-interest dominates much of the interaction. With narcissism, there may be occasional glimpses of agapic love, but they are often pushed aside by self-oriented drives.

We should keep in mind that Partners A and B may discover that their relationship cannot continue, not for lack of *agape* but because the requirements for fulfillment for each person are incompatible and cannot be met in a shared life. Despite their having a mutual love that is strongly agapic, life together will not work out. They cannot thrive in the relationship and must part. Such partings may be sad, but they will not be bitter.

There remains another possibility. Partners A and B may compromise so that each gives something and gains something. Since Partner A and Partner B make their own choices, they may choose to work together toward the realization of their potentials in a way that accommodates the fulfillment of both. Here agapic love remains intact, and both partners are able to pursue an evolutionary path they consider adequate to their needs.

Beyond all the challenges of attaining a proper balance of *agape* and *eros* in real-life intimate love, there is the great truth that intimate love can and should be a powerful demonstration of the harmonious interaction of *agape* and *eros*. *Eros*-driven, self-fulfilling love can, at the same time, be a beautiful work of agapic love. The works of *agape* are those actions that promote the fulfillment of the loved one. In this case, the lover seeks to enhance the evolutionary fulfillment of the loved one through *eros*-driven gestures and expressive actions that also fulfill the lover. The loving actions of *eros* are simultaneously the expression of *agape*, with the intention of supporting and encouraging the loved one's evolutionary advance. This is a beautiful form of mutually supportive *agape* and *eros* in action.

The Love Experience

Philosophy and personal experience tell us that the world is suffused with the power of love. We are surrounded by this power, but it also permeates us from within. We feel love inside and out. The radiance of loving benevolence (*agape*) surrounds us and holds us, while, at the same time, we radiate that benevolence to others and become filled with its special sensations. Through this inner and outer fullness run streams of loving desire (*eros*), longings for union and fulfillment, which bring their own kind of pleasurable satisfaction.

As conscious beings, we have the privilege of being aware of loving and being loved and making free choices as to how we practice love. We are doubly fortunate in possessing the capacity to feel the wider suffusions of love created by communities. All communities are mixtures of benevolence and desire, and those communities that find the right balance of the two are special. At a time when the world is brimming with devouring hunger, jealousy, anger, and greed, it is hard to stay in touch with the love that underlies all. However, the lack of works of love in the world is a reality that must be faced. It is not pleasant to contemplate greed and the destructive actions to which it gives birth, but we must face these facts if we are to realize our hope for the creation of a world in which love prevails.

Part Two: Greed

Introduction

GREED IS FIRST AND FOREMOST
A DEFECT IN THE PRACTICE OF LOVE

> The nineteenth century is now fast sinking into the grave, and we all begin to review its doings and to think what character it is destined to bear as compared with other centuries in the minds of future historians . . .. What I say, then, is that the great attention paid to economical questions during our century has induced an exaggeration of the beneficial effects of greed …until there has resulted a philosophy which comes unwittingly to this, that greed is the great agent in the elevation of the human race and in the evolution of the universe . . .. The twentieth century, in its latter half, shall surely see the deluge-tempest burst upon the social order . . . upon a world as deep in ruin as that greed-philosophy has long plunged it.[48]
>
> —Charles Sanders Peirce

Recently, CNN aired a documentary series about the 1980s. The program presented a sequence of clips of the elite of the 1980s extolling the glory of unrestrained acquisition of wealth, maintaining that not only was it legitimate and legal, it was noble and formed the ground for good moral decisions. Greed, in other words, had become good. Pierce's prophecy had come true. Significantly, the fact that some of those same opinion-makers were eventually charged and found guilty of fraud and other forms of financial misconduct did nothing to weaken the influence of their philosophy of greed in the eyes of the public. In the movie *Wall Street* (1987) we are presented with a stunning restatement of what, nearly a hundred years before, Peirce had described as the philosophy of greed. Gordon Gekko proclaims that "Greed...is good. Greed is right. Greed works. Greed clarifies, cuts through and captures the essence of the evolutionary spirit....Greed for life, for money, for love, for knowledge has marked the upward surge of mankind." When we encounter such an unabashed promotion of greed that Peirce foretold, we are pulled up short in our discussion of love, for it is clear that greed, not love, dominates the social and political life of the modern world.

It may be said that the primacy of *agape* over *eros* has been the basis for all of humanity's great accomplishments. Its reversal—the primacy of *eros* over *agape*—accounts for our greatest mistakes, injustices, persecutions, and atrocities. The unconstrained primacy of *eros* is what we commonly call greed.

In a useful, albeit incomplete, historical summary, Peirce wrote that philosophers of the Platonic tradition saw the great principle of growth and fulfillment to be *eros*, and that it was Christianity, particularly as enunciated by John the Evangelist, that replaced *eros* with *agape*, thereby making it possible to understand the true nature of human fulfillment and cosmic evolution. But, he added, the new evolutionary philosophy of love has had a hard time holding its own against what he deplores as the "philosophy of greed," which excludes *agape* from the moral equation and replaces unselfish loving with selfish acquisition. This philosophy teaches that greed represents our primal instinct, and that it is the basis of the true redemption of the human race, for "intelligence in the service of greed ensures the justest prices, the fairest contracts, the most enlightened conduct of all dealings between men, and leads to the summum bonum, food in plenty and perfect comfort."[49] The philosophy of greed promotes the idea that, if you think when you make moral decisions there is nothing in it for you, think again. You are kidding yourself. There must be some hidden greedy motive, albeit unconscious to you, underlying all your decisions. After all, greed is fundamental to your nature, the drive behind all evolution, the final criterion for all human action. In this way, the philosophy of greed claims to have discovered the hard-nosed truth about our deepest nature, a truth that (we are told) we sense but are afraid to admit.

The philosophy of greed excludes *agape* from serious consideration. Nevertheless, greed makes an ostentatious display of false benevolence; it must do so, for people carry a deeply rooted agapic instinct that is not easily overridden. Contrary to what the philosophy of greed teaches, *agape*, not *eros*, is the foundation of evolutionary growth.

The philosophy of love was promoted not only by early Christianity but also by all the great religions of the world, which, like Christianity, have done battle with the philosophy of greed. Most began with the primacy of *agape*, but elements within their institutions eventually lost sight of that fundamental truth and adopted unrestrained *eros* as the primary force of life, clearing the way for self-interest and the abusive exercise of financial power and control, the pursuit of prestige, and hatred of the *other*. All the great religions have struggled continually to purge these destructive excesses from their core teachings of love.

Although the experience of religions demonstrates the problem vividly, it is a mistake to think of the issue as primarily religious. The corruption of the hierarchy of human values that follows inevitably from the abandonment of the primacy of *agape* is a problem in every area of human moral thought and action. Everywhere that greed or vicious self-interest dominates, terrible things happen on the personal, social, political, and cultural levels of human interaction. These dire consequences are even more evident today than they were in Peirce's time. The investigation of these consequences and the examination of their possible remedies is the concern of the remainder of the book.

Chapter 3: Global Greed

Greed is a global problem. It is found in every country and every sector of the world's population, in individuals and in institutions. It is such a widespread phenomenon that we are not surprised when we see it. The practice of greed involves a philosophy. The philosophy of greed is simple: greed is admirable, and self-interest is the preferred criterion for making moral decisions. The ravages of greed are felt in every culture and community, but when greed is voiced and held up for admiration in public discussion, it almost always presents itself under the guise of magnanimity. When stated in its true unadulterated form, it is not pretty. Unfortunately, the public at large tends to accept the mask of benevolence without batting an eye. That is why it is important to reveal the philosophy of greed as it is beneath the disguise and show it in its stripped down, repulsive form.

One of the great mysteries of the dominance of greed in the world is the fact that it is accepted and defended not only by those who stand to profit most from it, the rich and the powerful, but also the average person in average circumstances, and even the poor. This fact points strongly to the need to understand the unconscious psychological and social forces at work in institutions, communities, and cultures. The solution to the global problem will be greatly aided by what we can discover on this front. We must understand that greed is an emotional state and stance that seeks self-enrichment above all. Over a century ago, Peirce examined the philosophy of greed as it was promoted in the books on economics of his time, and we see a similar promotion of greed in the financial and political elite of the world powers in our time.

Global Greed: A Philosophical Perspective

Peirce identified evolutionary love or *agape* as the fundamental metaphysical driver of cosmic evolution. He examined *agape* on both the cosmic and the human level. On the cosmic level, *agape* is a force embedded in all existent things. It consists of a dynamic intention that, during evolution, each thing attain the greatest possible fulfillment of its potentials. *Agape* does not specify a detailed outcome, however. Because evolution involves an element of freedom and spontaneity at every step, the final outcome cannot be predicted. Whatever one may imagine the source of universal agapic love to be, it does not compel a specific outcome for evolution as a whole. This means that in the actual course of evolutionary events, there will be crushed possibilities and developmental backwaters, but these ostensibly failed experiments in evolution do not indicate a failure of agapic love, because, given this specific universe, each evolving thing will act spontaneously in specific ways, and in the end, will have taken its evolution as far as it can go.

Agape, as manifested in human moral life, exists in a participatory form. It always has the same urgent intention: that loved ones achieve their greatest possible realization. However, the application of these loving feelings in actual moral decisions is neither mechanical nor subject to strict rules. Human beings have the capacity to be reflectively aware that they are agents of love and capable of affecting evolutionary processes in the world. They must use this awareness to evaluate the circumstances of each conscious choice and determine, to the best of their ability, how to balance *agape* and *eros* in the moral event. This means applying the principle of the primacy of the agapic. If this principle were effectively applied in human decisions, on both the personal and the social level, the world would be transformed. But is this possible, and if so, how should it be approached? In addition to the difficulties created by the sheer complexity of the human situations to which the primacy of *agape* is to be applied, there is the deeper and more vexing problem of the tremendous power of the unconscious dynamics that influence every one of our moral decisions. How can we deal with power? It is not enough to discover and understand the fundamental philosophical principles involved in our moral decisions or to make a case for the rightness of the principle of the primacy of agapic love. We must also identify the forces that are brought to bear against us as individuals and social groups, forces that support the primacy of *eros* and oppose agapic love.

This is why, beyond the philosophic dimension of the operation of *agape* and *eros* in the world and in human life, we need further information if we are to make wise moral choices. We need to know more than the primacy principle and the complexity of the conditions within which the choices are made. We need to identify the dynamics that operate largely unconsciously on the personal and the social level. Unfortunately, Peirce did not take us very far in this direction. What is needed is a psychosocial vision that has a strong psychodynamic component, a powerful internal consistency, and a sociological applicability that fits the empirical facts.

Global Greed: A Psychosocial Perspective

Greed appears at every level of society, but special kinds of greed occur among the rich and the poor. Wherever it exists, greed is fueled by the fear of weakness and the danger of being wiped out by forces beyond one's control. In its drive to be safe, greed tries to accumulate enough wealth and power to defeat those forces, no matter what form they take. Of course, one can never achieve this kind of invincibility, and the longing to attain such security can never be satisfied. Having this unacknowledged fear in common, greed in the rich and greed in the poor are essentially the same but present differently to the world, because the unconscious psychosocial dynamics are different in each.

When greed takes hold of rich people who have succeeded in accumulating large amounts of money and power for themselves, it is manifested as an appetite for more and more and yet more, and a willingness to use whatever means are available to secure it. When greed takes hold of the poor, however, it is fueled by fear and anger. Greed is based on the terrible fear of being unable to survive. Their genuine needs are not being met, or perhaps they are balanced on the knife edge between just making it and falling into destitution. In this state of mind, the poor are flooded constantly by urgent desires to enrich themselves so they can meet the world's real-life demands. This fear-fueled drive often generates anger at the pain of their state and a sense that "the world" is not giving them what they so desperately need and ought to be made to "pay up." They resent those who have everything they need, particularly the rich. For some, this flooding of self-oriented desire due to deprivation leads to acts of greed. They will do whatever it takes to obtain what they need and push away all agapic considerations. In this way, the instinct to look after oneself urgently informs all their decisions, and they take any necessary measures to feel safe. *Agape* is extremely difficult to maintain in such circumstances, and it is easy to understand the dominance of self-oriented *eros* in many who find themselves in this position, so that those who, in such circumstances, still give *agape* its place are deservedly seen as heroic.

However, sometimes another development occurs. The poor envy the rich and unconsciously identify their own interests with the interests of the wealthy, developing a tendency to live vicariously through them. This creates a paradoxical scenario in which the poor become the means for the rich to become even richer. The poor believe the grandiose promises made by the rich to help them escape from their turmoil. The greedy rich say, "Give me the power, and I will solve all your problems. You know what a successful person I am. This proves that beyond doubt I am able to devise a way to save you." Thus, the rich present a convincing case to the poor: if they join in a revolt against the status quo, they will all be better off. The poor's dire need makes them vulnerable to the manipulations of the greedy rich, and they are tempted to give themselves over to their oppressors' tender mercies.

Even though the form greed takes in the poor seems to be different from that in the rich, it is fundamentally the same: the desire for self-enrichment overshadows and displaces *agape*. Desperate for a solution to poverty, they grasp at straws of hope in whatever corner they find them. This vulnerability to impulsive, short-term greed can be seen taking over various segments of the population in times of crisis. Any effective remedy for global greed must take this into account, recognizing that greed needs to be healed in both rich and poor—and in all those who live in between.

Buried deep within our genetic makeup lies the feeling that we are most secure when we live in groups of people who are like us in some way. Thus, we tend to feel safest with members of our families, with those who share our religion, those who are part of the same ethnic group, who are of the same race, who are citizens of the same country, and so forth. We tend to feel insecurity, or even fear, in the presence of those who are unlike us, who are different, alien—other. If the other does not resemble us genetically, socially, or culturally, does not look like us or speak like us or think like us or dress like us, we are instinctively on our guard. These differences are not objectively sound reasons to be fearful. Being wary and suspicious of the "other" is the result of eons of natural selection: the best means of survival is often to distrust the unfamiliar. It is difficult to override this instinct and learn to trust others based on present, concrete, real-life information. But the struggle to rise above such ancient conditioning is crucial to the practice of *agape*. If we automatically consider a person who is different a threat, for no valid reason, we will find it difficult to feel genuine agapic love for that person. Whether in the case of individuals, groups, societies, or cultures, the defeat of the instinctive fear of the other, just because they are other, is of supreme importance for the establishment of peace and cooperation. The more aware we become of the problem of the fear of the other, the more readily we can recognize and overcome its manifestations, and the more effectively we will be able to practice agapic love.

Issues of the Unconscious

Beyond the considerations mentioned above is a set of subtler psychosocial forces at work in relation to the philosophy of greed. They represent a dynamic that usually operates on a fully unconscious level. If we can recognize these forces, we will begin to understand why the philosophy of greed has made inroads everywhere in the world and why we are so naïve about the degree of its destructiveness. Our inability to clearly identify the unconscious motives that drive greed's agenda makes us vulnerable to its incursions.

If we are to build the tools to deal with the globally active philosophy of greed, we need to consider several issues: 1) The hidden, unconscious motivations at work in the operation of greed have been little studied. 2) Greed is not primarily an individual problem but rather a collective one: a manifestation of the unconscious desires of the global community, in which dynamically active collectivities (groups/societies/cultures) influence all events of human life and create a "consensus trance" into which their members are initiated from birth. 3) These collectivities inculcate certain beliefs and orthodoxies that all members hold, or are supposed to hold, including, often under the mask of benevolence, the philosophy of greed. 4) Communities often work to thwart the creative thinking and actions of their individual members. 5) It is unclear how cultures might slough off their rigid orthodoxies and destructive practices. 6) Whatever the solution to global greed may be, it will involve establishing the practice of evolutionary love as the ultimate goal of the human community at large. I would like to expand my thoughts about each of these issues.

1. Historically, our examination of unconscious dynamics and hidden motivations has focused largely on the individual. In the West, our discovery of the unconscious occurred only 250 years ago, and even though that may seem like a long time, actual study of the subject has, understandably, progressed slowly.[50] The process began with discoveries made by Franz Anton Mesmer in the 1770s and was given an important psychological turn with the brilliant insights of his pupil, the Marquis de Puységur, beginning in the mid-1780s. Progress in understanding the psychodynamics of the unconscious was quite slow until the 1880s, when Frederick Myers, Pierre Janet, and William James brought new creative insight and energy into the field. Then, with the introduction of Freud's revolutionary ideas, starting in the 1890s, and Jung's unique contributions relating to the collective unconscious in the early 1900s, the notion of the powerful, dynamic influences of the unconscious mind took deeper root in the culture of the West,[51] and the examination of unconscious motivation made a great leap forward. This psychological tradition came to be called psychodynamic psychology, and it assumed a dominant position in the practice of psychotherapy, which it continues to hold at present.[52] The psychodynamic perspective on human life has become so deeply woven into Western culture that it is difficult to imagine a time when we had no systematic knowledge of unconscious dynamics. It has become accepted as part of Western cultural tradition. However, the orientation of this tradition has been toward the individual, and the discipline has less to say about collective or group psychodynamics.

2. Groundbreaking advances have occurred in our understanding of the interplay of conscious and unconscious elements in the individual, but we

have barely begun to address the conscious and unconscious dynamic factors at work in groups, communities, and cultures, and much work remains to be done in that area if we are to expose the essence of the philosophy of greed and counteract its influence in the broader human community. Greed is not rooted primarily in individual psychodynamics, and we cannot deal with it successfully if we approach it as a problem of the individual that can be solved through individualistic therapeutic methods. Human beings live, grow, create, and carry on transactions with each other in a community context. We develop regional societies that take on certain characteristics as the result of unexamined, unconscious influences. The roots of the characterology and the specific sets of beliefs and values of any particular culture are not easy to comprehend. Cultures are nested within cultures, from the smallest (the family) to the largest (ethnic groups, countries, and groups of countries), the largest of all being the human community as a global reality. While cultures have their own identities, they are inevitably influenced by the larger cultures in which they exist, just as individuals are influenced by their neighbors and ethnic relatives. The dominance of the philosophy of greed in global culture is a collective problem, with deeply hidden unconscious motivations, and will be difficult to analyze because of the great diversity of the elements of our world community. If we are to subject entire cultures to psychosocial examination, we will need new tools capable of probing not only the deepest unconscious motives of the individual but also the unconscious of the collective understood in the broadest possible sense. We are only in the earliest stages of developing such tools.

Cultures exhibit what I have elsewhere discussed as group-mind trances. The cultural group is focused on its own way of looking at life and the world that has grown up during its history and shows a correspondingly reduced awareness of other ways of seeing things. It mobilizes its resources, conscious and unconscious, to preserve its way of life. Cultural group-mind trances operate everywhere, in all populations of the world, and they all resist ideas and forms of conduct that contradict their core beliefs.

At their most positive, cultures channel their members' current creative energies and work to preserve the achievements of the past. Those within the culture who carry out these tasks may be thought of as trance-keepers (in the sense they are the guardians of the culture's group trance), protecting the view of the world that has become common to its members. Each culture creates its own meaningful reality, which is a particular version of reality as seen from that culture's unique perspective. Trance-keepers work from within that construct and reinforce its acceptance. Because it is a cultural consensus based on limited perceptions of the world, it is mediated by a kind of censorship that filters out unacceptable thoughts and perceptions. This means the culture finds it difficult to deal with members who have, in some way or another, expanded their perceptions to include some unfamiliar or forbidden elements. These members may come to represent a threat to the culture, and in many instances, the keepers crush the creativity and originality of those members in an attempt to preserve cultural institutions unchanged. Nevertheless, in every culture, eventually, those arise who are unhappy with the intellectual status quo, the built-in hierarchies, and the power structures. In terms of the cultural trance, these are trance-breakers who have, to differing degrees, freed themselves from the influence of the ideas that have been built into the structures of the culture, and expressed their contrary ideas in some public way. The built-in limitations on the perceptions of the culture eventually lead to the application of pressure on all to maintain the culture's constrained view of reality. Psychological investigations teach us that we tend to see what we expect to see and miss the unexpected. For the most part, the culture's limitations are invisible to its members until some trance-breaker casts off this culture blindness and talks about it. Sometimes this can lead to innovations within the culture but not typically without a fight. Resistance to change is a characteristic of virtually all coherent groups.[53]

3. The dynamics within cultures tend to create cultural orthodoxies. These foundational "truths" are the result of decades or centuries of cultural evolution and are broadly accepted as "correct thinking." They are settled opinions that can be formulated precisely and identified clearly by the orthodox and unorthodox members of society. To be a member of the group, one must be a true believer who consciously holds and defends these opinions. Tests may be administered to discover and denounce aberrant thinking. These tests may be blatant or subtle. Here are some examples of the orthodoxies at work in North American society.

- Scientism: Any opinion pronounced true by science or a scientist is infallibly true, and adherence to it is respectable. Any opinion that is scientifically unproven or not subject to scientific proof is suspect and unacceptable. Anything that a scientist rejects must be considered nonsense, naïve, superstitious, or dangerous.

- Moneyism: The belief that only money can provide true security in this insecure world and that to gain financial security is the highest of human aspirations. While the desire for financial security is understandable, even laudable, when it pushes aside all other considerations and all other values, it is a problem. Moneyism is all about survival, and it secretly tugs upon the deepest of human fears, mortality, and values the quest for money above everything else.

- Greed: Moneyism is a close relative of greed. The philosophy of greed is also a cultural orthodoxy, but, unlike other orthodoxies that proclaim themselves publicly with pride, the philosophy of greed must disguise itself and sugar-coat its pronouncements. Although some espouse it and congratulate themselves on what they think are their superior talents (as witnessed in the subjects of CNN's *The Eighties*), they are rare, and such behavior is usually considered reprehensible.

These are but a few of the many North American cultural orthodoxies. Other examples are racism and patriarchy.

4. Because members hold that the culture's foundational beliefs and practices are so valuable, they will attack, oppose, or exclude those who reject the rules or refuse to subscribe to the culture's orthodoxies. Among those who often experience pressure to conform are many of the culture's most creative people—artists, writers, original thinkers, and practical innovators. They are "outsiders," to use Colin Wilson's term.[54] Outsiders have strong agapic drives, and many express strong desires to advance the potentials of the world at large. Cultures that honor these individuals have been known to exist over the ages and throughout the world, but they are in the minority. As we shall see, the philosophy of greed tends to make life difficult for these original thinkers. If they are spared, it is often because the greedy find a way to use them for their own purposes.

5. In searching for the tools to deal with global greed, we are up against all the questions and challenges that face anyone trying to influence cultural groups. How and why do cultures increase their openness to new ideas and change? What causes them to entrench old ideas, and what means do they use? Is it possible to affect the dynamics in both instances? How do cultures infect each other, for good or for ill? What should leaders, rebels, innovators, and prophets do in these situations? What role can contemporary forms of communication play in the change processes? What part do threats and punishments play? What is the role of charismatic inspiration? These and many other questions come to mind when trying to visualize means of diminishing the culture-borne, global influence of the philosophy of greed in today's world.

6. The essential element in the struggle against the philosophy of greed is encouragement of the primacy of evolutionary love in human affairs. In practical terms, this involves working toward a balance of *agape* and *eros* in moral decision making. For this approach to be effective, knowledge of the true nature of *agape* must be disseminated globally.

Narcissism and Psychopathy

Before moving on, I want to draw attention to two psychological conditions that serve as impediments to the expression of evolutionary love: narcissism and psychopathy. I will not discuss their origins or whether and to what degree these syndromes are the result of genetic or environmental conditions. Rather, I want to examine the similarities and differences between them in terms of how they block or disrupt *agape*.

When talking about narcissism in this connection, I am referring more specifically to what is called narcissistic personality disorder—a pathology that produces a habitual preoccupation with oneself and anything that affects one's wellbeing. The narcissist looks at all conditions of life primarily in terms of self-interest, to such an extent that personal relationships of all kinds are seriously affected.

The narcissistic individual is not incapable of experiencing agapic love toward others, but agapic considerations are suppressed by self-centered considerations to such a degree that they hold only a small place in the individual's relationships. Also, although the narcissist is not incapable of sympathy with another, the ability to empathize with another or to "put oneself in the shoes" of another is easily swept aside by an overwhelming concern for self.

Psychopathic personality disorder is a more extreme disability that diminishes the chances of the individual experiencing agapic love to an even greater extent than narcissism. The psychopath is unable to feel sympathy for other human beings. He or she lacks what we expect to find in everyone—the ability to sense what the pain or discomfort experienced by another must be like and to feel sympathetic concern for that person's suffering. While the narcissist may occasionally or shallowly feel an instinctual sympathy for others, the psychopath is totally walled off from the experience and can only relate to it as an alien sentiment that others describe. The psychopath may learn to mimic the actions and expressions that are associated with sympathy but does not experience the feeling itself. Robert Hare, a world-recognized authority in matters relating to psychopathy, defines a psychopath as a person who is "without conscience."[55] Considering that *agape* is the conscience of *eros*, we can say that the psychopath is "without *agape*."

Does this mean the psychopath is doomed never to experience *agape*? It is difficult to answer this question. It is conceivable that a psychopathic person can feel and appreciate the unfolding of beauty in others or the world at large, and that this may evoke a feeling of agapic desire for the continued actualization of potentials he notices. It is possible, for instance, that a psychopathic personality can feel *agape* in the presence of a work of art or an awesome manifestation of a natural wonder. But insofar as *agape* may be experienced through a sympathetic appreciation of another person as a person, it will be unavailable to a psychopath.

To understand how to deal with the philosophy of greed in its global manifestations, I want to discuss its entrenchment in the many forms of human community. Human communities express themselves in many ways, one of which is that of revered cultural institutions. Unfortunately, these institutions can become breeding grounds for greed. In the next chapter, I examine two such institutions to discover what aspect of community life explains this vulnerability.

Chapter 4: Institutionalized Greed

The philosophy of greed has found a ready home in the institutions of human social life. For our purposes, it is useful to examine human communities from the perspective of their ability to open themselves to influences, from within and from without, that can lead to productive change. For this reason, before moving on to consider specific instances of greed in our major institutions, I want to examine communities in general to see how creative ideas are generated or retarded in their environments.

Natural and Interpretive Communities

Ideas are important. They are the precursors of our actions, and they determine what those actions will be. In a community, the flourishing of ideas is a sign of social health and leads to prosperity. Peirce tied the free flow of ideas to *agape*, giving as one of his principal examples of love our human ability to cultivate ideas "as we would the flowers in our garden." Ideas evolve and grow just as we do, and like us, flourish when given loving care.

The free and creative flow of ideas is a sign of mental health. Emotional disorders inevitably choke off ideas, creating rules and taboos about what thoughts and emotions can be allowed into the disturbed consciousness. The free flow of thought is essential to the free expression of feelings and the removal of stifling inhibitions in our interactions with others. Emotional disorders exist on both the individual and collective level of human living.

It is largely the community that determines whether free and creative thinking will thrive. Our thinking develops mainly through interaction with others. So, whether in a family or another form of culture, repression of free thinking has a devastating effect. The solution to the problem of global greed can only be found in an atmosphere of creative thinking, one that goes beyond the conventional. Reflective thought is greed's greatest enemy. Reflective thought reveals greed's true nature and exposes its ugliness. Reflective thought rips off greed's disguises and leaves it no place to hide. *Agape* and greed move in opposite directions. Greedy thinking collapses in the face of *agape*. Its cogency is destroyed when considered in the light of love. This is why the solution to the problem of global greed is dependent in part on the creation of spaces in which the free development of ideas is encouraged. Such spaces can only come into being in communities.

Some communities promote free thinking, and others discourage it. Robert Corrington gives us a useful starting point for examining this issue in his distinction between natural communities and interpretive communities.[56] He suggests that all human communities might be considered coherent webs of human interaction that possess a common purpose or telos. Natural communities are the normal and expected outcome of groups of human beings coming together to interact with each other. People join together because of their need for each other. They need each other to make various important things happen: to provide secure places for families to live, to obtain food, to improve living conditions, and to pool knowledge and skills that may benefit community life. And they need each other just for companionship. Natural communities exist to satisfy these needs, and they develop ways to do so—words and practices through which they communicate about how to cooperate in these tasks.

The appellation "natural community" is applicable not only to larger or longer-lasting communities with their unique cultures but also to smaller, more transient communities. Even the smallest communities tend to develop a peculiar "culture." Families are natural communities, as are religious congregations, government bureaus, and sports franchises. The great institutions of human culture are also natural communities. These include religious and academic institutions, as I will discuss later.

The importance of natural communities is evident. They have been central to life for as long as human beings have existed. Some natural communities that we encounter today have endured for long periods of time. These communities developed characteristic cultures or ways of thinking and acting, and these patterns have been handed down through the generations. The inheritance of wisdom and practical skills from previous members is of great value to natural communities. These ways of perceiving, thinking, and acting became community habits, and they are valuable habits, for they ensure that new each generation does not have to find out by trial and error what works and what does not. The cultural practices of natural communities are revered, and great pains are taken to preserve them and pass them on. These ways of being are generally not subject to question, for questioning might bring about change, and that change might cause the community to lose what it considers most valuable: the riches of its culture. The new tends to be feared. After all, these cultural practices have made it possible for the community to survive and even thrive. Attempts to introduce new practices could destabilize the community and jeopardize its existence. This state of affairs accounts for the powerful conservatism one finds in natural communities.

Corrington points out that natural communities give us our basic parameters for being in the world. They hark back to "the conditions of our origin," to our "whatness" in terms of race, class, gender, language, religion, and aesthetics. Through the community, we develop awareness of our cultural inheritance and the ideas from which we form "our collective identity and membership in our tribe." He tells us that

> this membership is exclusivistic and primal. It functions quietly and smoothly for the most part, giving us stability and a kind of semiotic warmth that protects us from the threat of meaninglessness and despair. Our natural communities are inert and locked in place—they reiterate the vast ancient conditions of origin, of law and rules of membership that exclude all non-tribal selves and which do so through a powerful demonization and abjection of Otherness.[57]

Otherness is dangerous. Otherness introduces the different, the unfamiliar; it threatens the tribe's safe and accepted worldview. The natural community has no room for new interpretations of reality or novel perspectives on the world in which we are immersed. Natural communities do not promote a climate of free thought. The natural community has a primitive instinct that discourages the exploration of ideas.

It is not hard to feel sympathy with the great pianist Glenn Gould, who, when speaking of the natural community that performers call "the audience," said, "I detest audiences—not in their individual components, but en masse I detest audiences. I think they're a force of evil. It seems to me rule of mob law."[58] Many of the most creative and original contributors to humanity's evolutionary advance have harbored similar sentiments. The drive to conformity in the natural community can be inexorable, destroying all in its path. Many theorists of the creative process have decried the harsh social forces that deny freedom to the evolving individual. This is the insight that led Colin Wilson to write his powerful study of the "outsider" as the epitome of the creative personality.[59]

It is essential to human evolutionary progress that dynamic realities oppose the repressive power of the natural community. This counterforce is found in what Corrington calls the "interpretive community." Interpretive communities encourage creative freedom and novel perspectives, thereby enriching the resources available to community members. The presence or absence of openness to new possibilities provides the principal criterion for distinguishing between a natural community and an interpretive community—or community of interpretation or community of interpreters. Corrington's term ties true creative freedom to originality in interpreting the signs by which we communicate with our fellow community members and through which we interact with the world at large. Here he references Peirce's notion of "semiotics"—the science of signs. Peirce says that we live in a world that is "profuse with signs" and that we constantly interpret the signs we encounter and become changed in the process.

Corrington tells us that a community of interpreters cracks open the standard, traditional meanings of familiar signs in the natural community, reinterpreting them and thus creating new spaces for community members to encounter novel ideas and practices. An interpretive community is characterized by a continuous reevaluation of experience that moves the human community forward but never reaches a final and complete formulation. Not only does the interpretive community create these "semiotic spaces," it also applies its critical powers to the natural community itself, questioning its "official" interpretation of reality. It recognizes that the natural community's standard worldview is, in some cases, corrupt and destructive of the freedoms of those it was meant to serve. The natural community, feeling itself under attack, may react by attempting to repress these outbreaks of interpretive freedom, rightly recognizing the danger they pose to the status quo. Religious and academic institutions may present themselves as interpretive communities, where personal freedom and creative thinking are welcome. But, as we shall see, they are natural communities, through and through.

Where does an interpretive community come from? It arises from within an extant natural community and remains within that community as it does its work. It comes into being when the right conditions are realized. Historically, philosophy has tended to develop in cultures in which a certain class of its members have sufficient leisure time to devote their attention to understanding the basic questions of human existence and the nature of the world. Corrington's view is that if an interpretive community is to come into being, "there needs to be a certain quantum of surplus energy left over after all instrumental needs have been met by a sufficient number of members of a given natural community."[60] Often this does not happen, because the community needs all its energy just to establish a workable and safe environment for its members and to take care of their survival needs.

While natural communities form hierarchical power structures to control the investment of community resources, interpretive communities tend to be more democratic. They generate mutual respect among members on the basis of their ability to initiate exploratory processes and freely seek out new and original ways of seeing things. They value the "original" individual who does not approach things from the community's traditional perspective but is engaged with unexpected possibilities. Ideas are generated that open undreamed-of vistas and invite further exploration, suggesting new ways of illuminating the world. In this way, members intellectually stimulate each other to break through to the new.

An interpretive community begins when a few people begin to question the natural community's established opinions, no longer taking it for granted that they are beyond criticism or critical evaluation. A certain amount of iconoclastic thinking is allowed, even encouraged. Members of the burgeoning interpretive community support each other in breaking new ground.

They take pleasure in fresh ideas and communicate their discoveries to each other. From this, they create a new community spirit, different from that of the natural community in which they are operating. It is a feeling of comradeship based not on familiarity and the security of traditional beliefs but rather on a shared sense of adventure into the unknown and the anticipation of the thrill of discovery.

Of course, this kind of community spirit is not likely to be appreciated by the authorities of the existing natural community. For this reason, interpretive communities tend to have a dubious status within the larger group and often experience a diminished sense of acceptance. Once formed, they may soon be denied the resources of the broader community. They may be shunned and or even persecuted by the members of their natural community. Sometimes an interpretive community can be shut down in a subtle, indirect, but effective way by a gradual reabsorption into the broader community. This can be done by sidelining or smothering new ideas with conventional thinking or by co-opting members of the interpretive community with offers of power or security, tempting them away from their new commitments and rewarding them when they agree to return to the fold.

What kind of natural communities can give rise to an interpretive community? It seems to me that the natural community must have a large enough population to support the formation of a smaller community within it. The interpretive community must be large enough to generate a significant output of creative perspectives and diverse enough to support an effective cross-pollination of ideas. For this reason, families, religious congregations, and similar small groups are unlikely to spawn their own interpretive communities. In these smaller contexts, one or two individuals may free themselves sufficiently from the power of the community to generate new or unconventional ideas, but this is not the equivalent of a community, with its complex web of relations and its identifiable common telos or goal.

Members of an interpretive community do not have to live in the same city or region. They may be geographically spread out and even have members around the globe. They can be "neighbors" in the sense described by Peirce: "'Our neighbor,' we remember, is one whom we live near, not locally perhaps, but in life and feeling."[61] This kind of association is even more relevant in our age of worldwide electronic communication. The realization that interpretive communities may or may not be geographically concentrated is important to keep in mind as we continue our exploration.

I would like to point out another difference between a natural community and an interpretive community, one that Corrington discusses under the rubric of eschatology. He notes that one way natural communities control their members is though envisioning a future in which the fundamental values of their community will be universally embraced, and its members will be chosen specifically to participate in the joys that will ensue in that transformed world. In its secular form, this transformation will be an idealized utopian version of the present community. In its religious form, it foretells the coming of apocalyptic end times, when divine power will intervene to destroy the community's enemies. This vision is used as a goad to members to remain true to the community's beliefs in anticipation of the great day of world transfiguration. The utopian visions of interpretive communities also promise societal transformation, but of a different kind. Members are offered the liberating opportunity to be part of a future community of creative freedom.

Many people today dream of belonging to a true interpretive community, in which they are free to explore their (often culturally unorthodox) ideas. We see attempts here and there to form such communities, with varying degrees of success. The most successful are those where the ideas of all are treated with respect, and there are no axes to grind or grand platforms to erect. Those who desire to form such a community must remember that the establishment and maintenance of a truly democratic attitude about communication and genuine deep respect for fellow members is extraordinarily difficult.[62]

Two Institutions

Over the centuries, many large natural communities have established institutions to carry out significant projects. In what follows, I examine two of them to cast light on how the philosophy of greed has established a place of dominance in the modern world. It is crucial to explore the psychosocial dimension of this phenomenon. This means seeing how the dynamics of natural communities, by their very nature, tend to offer an opening to greed and allow members to develop a philosophy that justifies its promotion.

Religious Institutions: The Betrayal of Spirituality

In this section, I describe religious institutions and their vulnerabilities to the philosophy of greed. In taking up this perspective, I do not intend to minimize or question the importance of religions and religious communities. They are worthy of the highest praise, respect, and admiration, and there is no doubt about the outstanding services they have performed for people everywhere. Nor is this inquiry intended as a criticism of religious people or religious ideas. Religions touch people's hearts and draw out the best in them. The analysis that follows in no way contradicts these incontrovertible facts.

In this discussion of greed in religious institutions, I need to start with a note about my understanding of some key terms.

First, what is a religion? In the definition offered by Jeffrey Kripal in his penetrating study *Comparing Religions*, a religion is: "any set of established stories, ritual performances, mind disciplines, bodily practices, and social institutions that have been built up over time around extreme encounters with some anomalous presence, energy, hidden order, or power that is experienced as radically Other or More."[63]

Kripal's definition gives us what we need for the present inquiry: a basis for understanding and thinking about religion that is as free as possible from defining the beliefs and structures of any specific religion.[64]

A religion is a community insofar as its members share common beliefs and common religious practices. The purpose or telos of that community is determined by its unique religious strivings. The purpose is what moves the community members in a common direction; that is, to promote, preserve, and protect the community and its beliefs and practices, and it is the glue that holds it together.

A religion is a natural community. A natural community is one that arises spontaneously in response to common needs. As a natural community, a religion carries within it all the propensities ascribed to natural communities in the first section of this chapter. Like all natural communities, they (1) take measures to protect their integrity and preserve their existence, and (2) strive to increase their membership and attain prosperity. History shows us that, in carrying out their purposes, religious communities can exhibit extreme greed, demonstrating a voracious appetite for power and money. Again and again, the drive for self-preservation and unlimited growth has spawned persecutions, massacres, torture, and wars for territory. In this way, the characteristics exhibited by natural communities can lead a religion into practices that are at odds with their founding intentions.

Religious communities are initially established around a set of beliefs, often formed in the presence of unusual experiences, and frequently involving a charismatic leader. The community comes together to promote and celebrate their beliefs and to do so in safety.

Typically, a religious community takes form outside the mainstream of social life in the region in which it arises. Its members band together for companionship, support, and security. A community culture develops and begins to codify beliefs and practices. As the community grows stronger, and its culture solidifies, it moves to clarify and expand the forms of expression it has created for its beliefs and to define them more precisely. It increases its sense of ownership and asserts its right to codify its leading features. Eventually, it manifests a protective attitude about those formulations. These developments are characteristic of natural communities generally.

The community creates structures that increase its power as well as the power of those who are in the upper echelon of its developing hierarchy. This power is used to protect the community's gains. Codes of belief, conduct, and practice become more rigid. Tests of orthodoxy are worked out. Fear of the unorthodox increases. The unorthodox are cast out, punished, or executed.

At this stage, the religious community may become apocalyptic in spirit, seeking to use any means available to establish the kingdom of heaven on earth. It may see itself as the hand of God, divinely empowered to make this happen. By this time, it has so entrenched its beliefs, practices, and rituals and so bolstered its inner authority that it feels justified in imposing its laws on all members and using its decrees to mobilize members to fight other communities with other beliefs. Those who profess variant beliefs within the religious community may be targeted as instruments of evil. Sub-communities within the larger religious group may make war on each other, each seeking to impose their will and their interpretation of orthodoxy.

A religion can exist as either a widespread or a local phenomenon. If its beliefs and practices spread to the far corners of the globe, various local communities (or sub-communities) within the global religion are likely to exhibit variations in beliefs and practices. However, as long as those peculiarities do not involve a radical departure from the broadly accepted creed, the religion considers the members of such communities to be their brothers and sisters. In any case, whether global or local, all religious communities are natural communities, and today all the great religions of the world have a global reach.

When a local religious group comes into being within a larger religious community, it may be because of 1) missionary effort, 2) political forces that fracture the larger group, or 3) the formation of an interpretive community within the natural community. When an interpretive community arises, it may decide to separate from the larger community not just in outlook but also geographically. Histories of religions show that reform groups frequently spring up and separate from the main body. However, not all reform groups qualify as interpretive communities. Some come into being because of power struggles or for other socio-political reasons.

A reform movement cannot be considered a genuine interpretive community unless it creates "semiotic space" around the community's beliefs and practices, as traditionally defined, and produces new perspectives and fresh ideas. It must maintain this spirit of open inquiry over time, and it cannot be considered an interpretive community if it questions orthodox forms, only to replace them immediately with a different set of equally rigid beliefs and practices. Some reform groups have had the true interpretive community's veneration of the spirit of intellectual freedom as an essential value and a proven ability to sustain themselves for a reasonable length of time. Every major religion has spawned such movements from time to time, but whether they were interpretive communities is a question that can only be answered by studying a wide range of such movements. It may turn out that genuinely interpretive communities have been few in number. In the absence of a thorough examination of the historical record, I am unable to venture an informed judgment on this matter.

When religions, as natural communities, set up structures to preserve their creeds and practices with the purpose of protecting, maintaining, and strengthening their core group, they may cease to be movements and become institutions. History indicates that once a religious institution achieves a certain degree of power and concomitant financial resources, it is in danger of becoming an aggressive force. The actions taken by religious institutions regarding their own members and their neighbors and rivals can be ruthless. At this point, the religious institution is practically incapable of extending agapic love in the true sense of the word. There is no chance for unconditional love to be the chief determinant of the institution's actions. It acts to ensure the security, continuity, growth, prosperity, and permanence of its community. The love that dominates and motivates it as an institution will be some form of *eros*, and frequently an *eros* acting largely without the restraint of *agape*.

It should come as no surprise that religious institutions easily become a welcoming home for the philosophy of greed, particularly if the accumulation of power and financial resources for the purposes of survival and strengthening takes primacy over all other considerations. When a hierarchical structure is in place, those who are chosen to direct the religious community's policies and decide its actions quickly come to see themselves as superior representatives of the institution and have little difficulty appropriating for themselves a generous portion of its wealth and power. The group mind or group thinking that pervades the institution, both consciously and unconsciously, tends to create an inflated view of the leaders' importance, and many of them show themselves more than ready to accept the role of potentate. This creates ideal conditions for the entrenchment of greed. All group minds operate as social organisms, living things that influence the thinking and actions of its members. As organisms, they have the drive to protect themselves and grow, to subjugate the part to the whole. Some individuals or groups within the institutional hierarchy are genuinely capable of agapic love, but under the insistent pressures of the group mind, they will find it difficult to give that sentiment priority in their decisions. This is a particularly unfortunate state of affairs for religious institutions which, by their very nature, we expect to exemplify the highest motives and most elevated ideals.

The power of a religious institution's group mind is formidable. Frequently, it communicates contradictory messages, dissociatively blocking out one alternative or the other, depending on the context. For example, a religion may teach about agapic love in its holy books and at the next moment convey, consciously or unconsciously, to its members that they are perfectly justified in condemning those who disagree with the teachings of the religion and even applying emotional or physical force against them. The contradiction between these two teachings is hardly noticed, and this opens the door for members to direct hate toward others with no qualms of conscience. Here the unconscious message—a license to abuse—overwhelms any conscious doubts. This is not surprising, since psychodynamic principles indicate that unconscious motivations that continue unexamined have great power.

This two-level communication makes room for greed to establish itself, conveying, on an unconscious level, that the unrestrained accumulation of wealth and power, with no consideration for the good of others, is perfectly all right, even virtuous. Meanwhile, the beneficiaries of this greed make public protestations about the benevolence of their actions, seemingly unaware of their true motives. Members of the religious community develop a dissociative blindness to these contradictions and, as a result, there is little or no critical examination. Attempts to raise questions are ignored or treated as indications of a lack of faith.

When a religious institution succeeds in gaining power within a society's political structure, it may be able to introduce its established beliefs into governmental policies and attempt to privilege those beliefs in the law. In some cases, the religious institution may actually succeed in taking over the government. In such cases, the institution's established religious beliefs become civil law, and this makes them difficult or even impossible to challenge. Those religious authorities who gain power and influence in such a government's political and financial structures will encounter no bar to the practice of unbridled greed. Whether this greed accumulates resources to enrich privileged members of the institution or the community as a whole, it is still greed.

The fruits of greed can hardly be hidden in such a situation, so explanations and justifications must be offered for the concentration of the community's power and wealth in the hands of the few. These are soon formulated and tied in to the tenets of faith. In some instances, such unvarnished greed is resisted by leaders within the institution, but it is rare that such an attitude survives their term of office.

This greed-dominated situation may give rise to resistance in the form of an interpretive community within the religion's natural community. Such a community is unlikely to develop within the institution itself but may coalesce among the conscientious faithful. The members of the burgeoning interpretive community will question the institution's perspective and call for a deeper examination of ideas that have been generated to support the greed-ridden power structure. The religious institution itself can be counted on to oppose and condemn such questioning. In the face of repressive action, the community of interpreters will often back down and abandon their efforts. But in some instances, it may find a way to continue. Perhaps some members of the institution's power structure, despite opposing pressure from the establishment, encourage its efforts, and a groundswell of popular support may allow the community of interpreters to survive in difficult circumstances.

That religious institutions, which exist to uphold noble beliefs, can evolve into strongholds of greed is a fact of history and is still seen in today's great global religions. None of the world's religions have escaped the domination of the philosophy of greed, which has become a theology of greed. All the great religions have shown remarkable blindness to the moral contradictions they foster in their teachings on the practice of love. At some point, all of them have been guilty of the practice of hatred of those who differ in their beliefs, and their histories include the commission of incredible atrocities against their fellow human beings.

All the world's religions, if they are to be true to their spiritual core, must courageously face up to their histories and investigate how the philosophy of greed has infiltrated their institutions. Religions can teach the power of love to the world. It is a pity that love, especially *agape*, so seldom occupies the center of concern.

The University: The Commodification of Knowledge

> Suppose, for example, that I have an idea that interests me.
> It is my creation. It is my creature; for . . . it is a little person.
> I love it; and I will sink myself in perfecting it. It is not by
> dealing out cold justice to the circle of my ideas that I can
> make them grow, but by cherishing and tending them as I
> would the flowers in my garden.
>
> Charles Sanders Peirce[65]

The university would seem to be a natural home for the agapic love for ideas. Professors should be nurturers of creative and original thinking, experienced and attentive "gardeners" (in the sense meant by Peirce) cultivating intellectual continuity with the past and innovation for the future. Students in the seedbed of ideas should find inspiration in the great intellectual accomplishments of the past. However, the university has not escaped the infiltration of greed. Ambition for money and power threatens to become the driving motivation for professors and students and the overarching goal for administrators: the domination of *eros* over *agape*.

The university, understood as a "community of teachers and scholars" (*universitas magistrorum et scholarium*) took shape in the Middle Ages. Since then, it has undergone a rich and complex evolution. Until recently, it was a place of learning in non-vocational subjects. Now, according to many contemporary critics, it has become a vocational school, supplying trained employees to industry, with little emphasis on scholarship or the cultivation of a well-rounded grasp of the breadth and depth of human knowledge. In view of these critics, the original definition can be revised to "a community of teachers and apprentices to the workforce." This and other characteristic problems are products of the philosophy of greed.

Agapic love is directed toward all things. For Peirce, persons hold a unique place as objects of our love. But for him, "persons" were not just individual human beings or even human communities. Among what he considered persons, Peirce included ideas. Like human persons, Peirce argues, we give birth to ideas, love them, nurture them, and try to stay out of their way as they develop into the fullness of what they can become. Our love for ideas is, or should be, a benevolent love, without strings or conditions. Ideas must never be distorted, constrained, or suppressed for the sake of personal enrichment.

So, one is not surprised to hear that when Peirce discussed the state of the universities of his era, it was the welfare of ideas that preoccupied him. He sounded the alarm about the philosophy of greed in the university in an article he wrote for the journal *Science* in 1899. Reviewing a book published on the tenth anniversary of the founding of Clark University in Massachusetts, Peirce begins by observing that the average university trustee considers any professor who invests time and energy in theoretical research to be a "barely respectable squanderer of his opportunities."[66] Peirce vehemently opposes this stance. Insisting that a university exists to benefit the great human community, he writes: "The great medieval universities . . . were never in the least founded for their students' individual advantage, but on the contrary, because of the expectations that the truth that would be brought to light in such institutions would benefit the state."[67]

Peirce asserts that the only motive that drives a genuine scientist and scholar is to render things reasonable, "which consists in assimilation, generalization, the bringing of items together in an organic whole." He laments that what was actually happening in the American university of his day was something quite different. The main motivation for students, as touted by many universities, was supposed to be self-interest and self-promotion. He sees this as a perversion of what the university was meant to be, writing, "Surely the purpose of education is not different from the purpose of life." If happiness and fulfillment are the purpose of life, the goal of education can never be pure self-enrichment; it must be the pursuit of aspirations that take one beyond oneself: "No reader of this journal is likely to be content with the statement that the searching out of the ideas that govern the universe has no other value than that it helps human animals to swarm and feed. He will rather insist that the only thing that makes the human race worth perpetuating is that thereby rational ideas may be developed and the rationalization of things furthered."[68]

Thus, by Peirce's account, we know that, in 1899, the philosophy of greed had already established its hold on the universities. He is taking aim here not at the laudable and necessary practice of paying lecturers a living wage but at the elevation of money and acquisitiveness as the academy's primary goal. Ideally, universities should be interpretive communities that, in turn, encourage further sub-communities of interpretation. However, universities cannot help but be, in the first place, natural communities, with their own set of interests to promote and protect. Because of their position of trust in the human community, universities should nonetheless be aware of the ideal—the creation and furthering of communities of interpretation—and augment their efforts to create the conditions for free and original thinking. Unfortunately, examples of such encouragement of ideas are less frequent than one might hope. Nevertheless, universities are among the few institutions today that still have the genuine capacity to create influential interpretive communities.

Present-day critics of the university echo Peirce's lament for the demise of integral learning in favor of an accumulation of knowledge for the sole purpose of maximizing financial gain. Thomas Docherty puts the issue this way:

> There is a war on for the future of the university worldwide. The stakes are high and they reach deep into our social condition. On one side are self-proclaimed modernisers who view the institution as vital to rational economic success. Here the university is a servant of the national economy in the context of globalization, its driving principle of private and personal enrichment necessary conditions of "progress" and modernity. Others see this as a radical impoverishment of the university's capacities to extend human possibilities and freedoms, to seek earnestly for social justice, and to participate in the endless need for the extension of democracy.[69]

Today, the ideals embodied in the academy are in danger. The philosophy of greed has insinuated itself into educational policies in two areas:

1. The promotion of a hunger for money and power over the desire for knowledge and wisdom as a life goal for students.

2. The promotion of a hierarchical power structure that allows faculty to exercise arbitrary authority over what ideas will and will not be considered acceptable in their various fields of expertise.

Regarding the first area, many universities' promotional materials now include glowingly worded descriptions of greed for financial gain among their stated goals and proclaim that ambition to the world, their students, and their benefactors. With regard to the second area, faculty who are in positions of power and influence are too often happy to adjudicate which ideas and attitudes are to be approved as orthodox and true. This arbitrary curtailing of intellectual exploration limits the possible directions of study or research to be pursued, affecting both students and faculty. Students are affected, in that opinions that contradict the orthodox stance are either not taught or are taught only in a cursory and dismissive manner. Faculty are affected by the de facto reduction of their ability to freely express and teach their own views on the matters at stake.

The issue of tenure plays a crucial role in the enforcement of the locally determined orthodoxy. Tenure is the promise of lifetime employment to those who complete a probationary period. During that time, the writing, research, and general character of professors are scrutinized by their colleagues to assess whether they deserve this privilege. Tenure was instituted after the Second World War when potential university faculty were in short supply. At the time, the introduction of tenure was intended to attract the most qualified people by promising them the security of a permanent position and thus to enhance the quality of research done in the university. However, now in a time of oversupply, in many cases it has the opposite effect. It has ensured that candidates hoping to be admitted to the university's permanent staff will not challenge whatever orthodoxy is currently in vogue in the departments to which they belong. In this way, the system imposes a form of censorship that effectively blocks any ideas except those of tenured faculty. It also tends to produce professors who cease to grow intellectually once they are securely tenured and know their future is assured, while non-tenured faculty are careful to keep clear of expressing any original, creative, but "unorthodox," ideas lest they ruin their chances of a permanent position. Unfortunately, it is a common subject of conversation among the untenured that they are waiting until after the conferral of tenure to do the writing and research that really excites them.

Beyond the negative effects of how tenure operates today, other practices have similar consequences. Among them are peer review and publication requirements. These factors are in place for graduate students and instructors long before there is any question of tenure, and they are concerns that make themselves felt for students in, for example, issues relating to applications for grants, early hirings, and post-doctoral research positions. In all these areas, although matters of uncensored intellectual freedom and thriving creativity are not related directly to money, the indirect connection is always there. Hidden pressures to conform strengthen the links between influence and income, further entrenching the dominance of orthodoxy.[70]

I take seriously Peirce's notion expressed in the quotation given at the beginning of this section that ideas should be considered persons and that we should cherish and tend them as we would our children, our friends, or the flowers in our garden. Ideas, according to this view, are singularly unique human creations, and if they are arbitrarily censored, summarily dismissed, or crassly commodified, we must count them among the greatest and most tragic casualties of the growing domination of the philosophy of greed in universities.

A reformation is required. In universities, the philosophy of greed must be replaced by the philosophy of agapic love, the love that creates and unifies. Peirce wrote, "The movement of love is circular, at one and the same impulse projecting creations into independency and drawing them into harmony,"[71] and noted, when writing about ideas, that "the Law of Love and the Law of Reason [the pursuit of ideas] are quite at one." [72]

Part Three: *Agape* And Human Evolution

But already my desire and my will were being turned like a wheel, all at one speed, by the Love which moves the sun and the other stars.

—Dante, *The Divine Comedy, Paradiso*, Canto XXXIII, lines 142–145 (translated by C.H. Sisson)

To love agapically is the human being's single-most primitive instinct. Here I am not using the word "instinct" in a biological sense but as a description of the force that creates a feeling, accompanied by the urge to act on that feeling. The feeling is the passionate desire for the loved one to grow. The urge to act is the posture of readiness to support this growth. In human beings, *agape* is a conscious attitude and the primary guide for deliberately chosen actions. The instinct to love agapically cannot be excised or destroyed, for that would mean removing something fundamental to human existence.

Agape can, however, be suppressed, but its suppression requires a kind of violence. Such violence is applied by elements at work in the inner and outer environments of the morally active person. Once these suppressing conditions are removed, *agape* springs into action, like a stretched spring snapping back into place. Discovering the means for disarming these suppressive forces will allow *agape* to be re-established in its rightful position of primacy in the moral life of individuals and communities.

Chapter 5: *Agape And Hope*

The Human Condition

Human beings are in a difficult position. We are placed at the intersection of the world of existing things and its ineffable source. In the course of our evolution, we have gradually become more conscious of our position and more capable of making choices about our actions in the world based on knowledge. Had we no reflective consciousness, we would live out our lives from habit. We would automatically feel the push of *agape* urging us to activate our potentials, and our interactions with the world would largely follow the patterns that have proven to be successful over eons. Even without self-questioning, we would follow our desires for growth and enrichment, doing our best to survive and prosper.

But we *are* consciously reflective beings, and we are not destined to live lives of such simplicity. For not only do we feel the push to evolve, which comes to us from cosmic *agape*, we also have the experience of *agape* as a feeling state of our own. We love the world with a cosmic love, and we cannot avoid knowing that our choices affect the world for good or ill. We can make decisions that enhance the growth of others, or we can choose to do things that retard or destroy that growth. Whether we like it or not, we have been made shepherds of the world, looking after the welfare of those existent things in our orbit of influence—whether they be ideas, the environment, living creatures, or other human beings with whom we share this unique place in nature.

The human race did not ask to be put into this position. It simply evolved, and we have only gradually awakened to our destiny. We must look after our own welfare—that is our duty—but also the welfare of everything we affect. It is a seemingly impossible task, for we feel daunted by the prospect of having to gain enough knowledge and generosity to do a good job.

We feel this way, because we are in the early stages of the process and cannot see ahead very well. At present, we are strongly preoccupied with the urge of *eros*, the urge that says, "Engage and enrich yourself!" The primacy of *agape* is still not well established. This why greed is so dominant in our world. The development of consciously integrated *agape* is still in its infancy. Our intellectual abilities have far outstripped our capacity for agapic love, and we see great vistas of technological discoveries that seem to invite us to have more, more, and yet more. We are like hungry children let loose in a candy store, running from delight to delight, filling ourselves to the utmost, heedless of the fact that all these sweet things do not really belong to us and not realizing how sick they will make us feel.

How are we going to grow up and move beyond this childlike stage, so vulnerable to greed and excess? How are we to strengthen the presence of cosmic *agape* in our feelings and doings? We see signs here and there of those who are already stepping into the coming age of *agape*. We marvel at the tales of benevolence, loving consideration of others, sympathy, and selfless-ness that we hear of now and again. And we sense that, in some cultures, pockets of thriving *agape* have sprung up here and there over the centuries. It has started to dawn on us that perhaps we can do something to accelerate this new step on humanity's evolutionary path. The advance guard of *agape* is stirring and making itself known.

Many are coming to see, however, that this advance cannot be accom-plished merely by introducing new and creative ideas or schemes and trying to apply them from the top down. People can be inspired by visionary pro-grams, and they may see their cogency and attractiveness, but the application of these programs cannot be sustained. A truly sustainable advance must be built up from the roots, and, for humanity, the root is community.

One Reality

The work begins with the recognition that we are not really a multiplicity of "I's" who have to find a way to pool our resources, isolated little "I's" that, in loneliness and desperation, need to find each other and form bonds of common purpose. The truth is that there is only one "I" that acts through us all. There is only one "I," the "I" we find twinkling everywhere in the great tapestry of interconnectedness that is the world of humanity. It precedes us and continues after us. We need to discover that the "I" is already there, the consciously active factor in an indestructible, ever-changing, ever-evolving web of relations.

This is powerfully expressed in a novel by Muriel Barbery, in a passage describing a young woman's experience of singing in a musical choir:

> Every time, it's a miracle. Here are all these people, full of heartache or hatred or desire, and we all have our troubles and the school year is filled with vulgarity and triviality and consequence, and there are all these teachers and kids of every shape and size, and there's this life we're struggling through full of shouting and tears and laughter and fights and break ups and dashed hopes and unexpected luck—it all disappears, just like that, when the choir begins to sing . . .. So when they sing a canon I look down at the ground because it's just too much emotion at once: it's too beautiful, and everyone singing together, this marvelous sharing. I'm no longer myself, I am just one part of a sublime whole, to which the others also belong, and I always wonder at such moments why this cannot be the rule of everyday life, instead of being an exceptional moment, during a choir. When the music stops, everyone applauds, their faces all lit up, the choir radiant. It is so beautiful. In the end, I wonder if the true movement of the world might not be a voice raised in song.[73]

The idea of a deep communal oneness is an ancient one. Jeff Kripal says some traditions within the general history of religions "emphasize some "hidden" or "secret" communion, a connection or even complete identity, between human nature and the "really Real," however these two are conceived. Precisely because of this experienced unity or identity, mystical traditions generally emphasize sameness and downplay difference. Indeed, the most radical forms of mystical thought deny difference altogether, asserting that cultural, religious, and ethnic differences are entirely surface matters and that, deep down, we all share, we all are, the same Reality."[74]

We have forgotten that the world we experience is one unified, interconnected reality. Focusing on one aspect of the world and then another, we have ended up with pieces and lost track of the whole—and then we try desperately to paste the separate parts together to form some kind of unity. The world does not exist in pieces; it is a whole. No matter our feeling about it, that whole still stands, and it is only our dissecting intellect that creates the false impression of something fractured.

We have pulled the same sleight of hand with our view of ourselves. When we focus on our conscious thinking, we believe we are atomic units separate from each other. But when we become aware of our feeling experience, we have no such impression.

The mistaken impression we have of being isolated units brought together by happenstance enters any conversation we have about the individual and the community. Charles Peirce knew, better than most, the real nature of human individuality and human community. He tried, in perhaps an awkward and halting way, to talk about his vision in terms of what he called his philosophy of "synechism." Synechism means continuity, that everything is continuous with everything else. By continuity, Peirce meant to point directly to a oneness. He meant to refer to a oneness that does not easily lend itself to conceptualization or imaginative exploration. It is a oneness with its roots planted in the depths of nature beyond time and space, or before time and space, or having nothing to do with time and space. It is a oneness that we can only know by becoming truly aware of actually existing, by moving beyond ideas about ourselves and our lives to a point of feeling our existence and its real structure. This experience leads to the conviction that the world is one indivisible whole, a unified continuity.

Peirce's understanding of the one and the many in community has implications for how we see our own personhood. We are inclined to equate being a person with being separate, walled off from others. Speaking about the innumerable threads of communication constantly active among us, Peirce says, "You think there must be such isolation because you confound thoughts with feeling-qualities; but all observation is against you. There are some small particulars that a man can keep to himself. He exaggerates them and his personality sadly."[75]

Personality does not equal isolation. We are not separate things. We are not things at all. We are nodes in the network of relations that is humanity. Peirce tells us we must not say, "I am altogether myself and not at all you." Rather, our connections with each other and our contextualizing of each other are continuous and pervasive, because "all communication from mind to mind is through continuity of being."[76] Ideas are conveyed through a continuity of being, not through one isolated entity creating words and gestures that are transmitted to the sensorium of another, who then translates them back into ideas. That kind of process does happen, but it constitutes a mere trickle compared to the vast stream of communication that occurs constantly on the level of feeling.

The stream flows forward through constant communications, of which we are only partly conscious. The more conscious aspect shows itself in the ways we use language—written or conveyed through gestures or by means of images and artistic conveyances of all kinds. In this way, meaning is communicated and received. It is received in a perception that immediately summons an interpretation, one that transforms us, making us something we were not before. Then each of us, in our turn, continues the stream of communication, through our own forms of expression, to pass on an altered and newly enriched message to those in our orbit.

Another, perhaps more universal, way of looking at the transforming power of communications among the nodes of human society emphasizes the ubiquity and power of signs in the evolutionary growth of all of us, as individuals and as collectives. In this view, we are all in a constant flux of growth and enrichment through the transformative effect of encounters with signs. This goes beyond the discussion of communication as language and identifies the action of signs that are active not only in the communities formed by living things but also in the collectivities of everything that exists in the universe. This understanding of communities is fundamentally semiotic.

We might say that we have three kinds of consciousness and three corresponding ways of communicating: 1) our bodily consciousness, which is tied to our physical functioning and communicates largely through sense information, 2) our social consciousness, which is our awareness of and intercommunication with the total network of humanity in both individual and community nodes, through sheer continuity of being, and 3) our spiritual or cosmic consciousness, which exists at the point where humanity emerges into existence and which is the ultimate source from which we say "I" and the foundation of all of the communication that occurs among us.[77]

In the coming into existence of human beings, this cosmic consciousness is the first manifestation of *agape* and the means by which *agape* is embedded in human beings. It has been called many things, such as the Infinite Self and the Ultimate Self, but it is probably best known by its Hindu name, Atman.[78] When we experience *agape* manifesting in our feelings and intentions, we are most in touch with our deepest cosmic roots. When we feel this same *agape* manifesting in the rest of the human community, we know that the real basis for hope for humanity consists in learning, individually and collectively, to introduce felt *agape* into every human activity.

To recognize humanity as a community that experiences universal sympathy—this is the desired outcome. To see all individuals who comprise this universal web of relations as our brothers and sisters and to expand the concept of community beyond any location, beyond the concept of philia (benevolent community love), beyond any limitation—this will lead to the elevation of *agape* to its proper place in the world.

The Great Step Forward in Human Evolution

This takes us back to the question posed at the beginning of this chapter: How are we to enhance *agape* in the world and thereby dethrone greed from its position of global dominance? How are we to establish *agape* in its proper place as the conscience of *eros* in both individual and collective morality? How are we to take this next great step forward in human evolution? There are some signs that the realization of this desired future state is already in process in those who are working, as individuals and as communities, to find a way to practice this feeling awareness of *agape*. They are attempting to live this feeling concretely in practical life. To be successful, their practice must be an individual and a community undertaking, because humanity itself is both individual and communal, and the feeling that is being sought cannot be understood and put into practice without the participation of both.

We are fortunate in the West, for we live in a culture that has developed an indispensable tool for success in this project. This tool is a psychodynamic view of the human psyche. As I mentioned in Chapter 3, over two hundred years ago, the Marquis de Puységur discovered that there lies within us a region of thought, feeling, and intention that influences us without our being aware of its operations. This region is what today we call the "unconscious." Through the decades since then, our understanding of its dynamics and its relationship to our conscious life has grown considerably, to the point that we have been able to establish forms of "psychodynamic" psychotherapy that can significantly improve people's emotional lives.

Despite our progress, our knowledge is still in a primitive state. For one thing, we have developed only a rudimentary understanding of the personal unconscious. For another, Carl Jung's teachings about the collective unconscious give us a mere glimpse of what is yet to be learned about its origins, meaning, and power. Also, and very importantly, although we have spent a great deal of time exploring the dynamics of the unconscious in individuals, we know almost nothing about the unconscious dimension of group life. By groups I mean not only smaller collectivities, such as families and social groups, but also ethnic groups, societies, cultures, and nations, as well as the great collectivity of humanity. We remain almost totally in the dark about the unique unconscious dynamics of each of these levels of collectivity. This is one of the great areas of study I hope will be given more attention in the future.

Even so, we have some significant initial insights into the life of the unconscious and can build successfully on what we have discovered so far. This gives us considerable reason for hope. It stimulates our curiosity and the desire to increase our knowledge in this field to serve our work of enhancing the presence of *agape* in the great human collectivity.

But we should not pass lightly over the degree of ignorance we still labor under regarding the unconscious, especially regarding human communities. The enhancement of *agape* and the diminution of greed in the world can only be achieved by collective endeavor. In this matter, communities are both a source of problems and a great blessing for taking our great evolutionary step forward.

In Chapter 4, I discussed the dynamics of human communities in terms of natural and interpretive communities. Natural communities are a part of human life everywhere. They are formed to look after the needs of various groupings of people. Their strength is based on their common purpose, which brings the resources of the community together to support the community's interests. The weakness of the natural community is its tendency toward rigidity of thought and the formation of rules and rituals that stifle creativity, blocking energies that could be applied to devising new means for community prosperity. A strong conservative impulse is at work in all natural communities, as well as a tendency toward hierarchy. If innovation, creativity, and fruitful inventiveness are to be fully expressed, another kind of community structure must be established, one that allows and even rewards the free play of thought and experimentation in living. In other words, an interpretive community. Such a community will contain a certain amount of iconoclasm and rebelliousness, but, if allowed room, it will open rich and unexpected veins of possibility that can benefit all.

Peirce had something like this in mind when he wrote about his concept of a "Community of Inquirers." After talking about the constrictive, anti-creative state of affairs that arises from allowing limited personal or cultural interests to dominate our lives, Peirce points out that death soon puts an end to our endeavors, and we can ill afford to waste time in activities driven by such motives. The search for an understanding of the universe is the great project of humanity, he insists, and we must take a different road.

> It seems to me that we are driven to this, that logicality inexorably requires that our interests shall not be limited. They must not stop at our own fate, but must embrace the whole community. This community, again, must not be limited, but must extend to all races of beings with whom we can come into immediate or mediate intellectual relation. It

must reach, however vaguely, beyond this geological epoch, beyond all bounds. He who would not sacrifice his own soul to save the whole world, is, as it seems to me, illogical in all his inferences. Logic is rooted in the social principle . . .. But all this requires a conceived identification of one's interests with those of an unlimited community.[79]

Peirce sees such a community as a self-correcting source of knowledge influenced by a rich cross-pollination of ideas. The result will be a convergence on truth that advances over an indefinitely long period of time, a progressive evolution during which failed hypotheses are thrown out and more successful ones are installed.

Agape is enhanced in such a community, since ideas and visions of life are cultivated, as Peirce said, like flowers in a garden, and allowed to develop into new and unexpected forms of human life. We have seen that greed can easily take hold of natural communities whose structures are rigid and whose rules are draconian. Interpretive communities, on the other hand, encourage and embody agapic love toward people and ideas. Communities that set out to promote the knowledge, feeling, and practice of *agape* will naturally have the structure of interpretive communities. Here freedom and mutual respect are prized. Means for combatting prejudice about individuals and bias about ideas are put in place. Self-reflection on both the individual and the community level are the norm for communal life. This entails a readiness to consider things psychodynamically, acknowledging the presence of unconscious influence on both levels.

In today's world of immediate communication over the Internet and by other electronic means, interpretive communities need not exist in a particular locality. As Peirce said, "'Our neighbor,' we remember, is one whom we live near, not locally perhaps, but in life and feeling."[80] Current technology significantly expands our neighborhoods and removes the limits imposed by physical distance.

We promote this freer and more open attitude toward new ideas and new practices in various ways. One of them is to appreciate those cultural trance-breakers,[81] who are struggling to remain open and explorative in the face of disapproval and opposition from the natural community. Colin Wilson recognized the important role of these people in his ground-breaking book, published over fifty years ago, *The Outsider*.[82] Outsiders are in the vanguard of discovery in a culture. They see things from new perspectives and can give expression to their renegade visions in the arts and other forms of communication. The term "outsider" does not refer to such persons' attitudes toward social life. The outsiders that Wilson describes may or may not enjoy the company of others. They are outsiders, because they can stand outside the limitations of awareness imposed by the culture, challenging their culture's standard way of seeing things. Some of them also become outsiders in the sense they are ostracized by their culture and made to live on the fringes of normal social life. Such outsiders are put in the position of the alien or other and deemed deserving of ridicule and exclusion. In some cases, they are imprisoned, tortured, or even executed—testimony to the lengths to which a natural community will go when it decides to remove an element it considers threatening to the status quo.

I do not want to give the impression that interpretive communities and outsiders merely develop and explore ideas. Ideas alone are not enough to affect the enhancement of *agape* and the diminution of greed. What must be encouraged are feelings and holistic forms of engagement with the world. To accomplish this is a greater task than teaching ideas. It involves overcoming powerful habits, ingrained ways of responding to the world as a person and as an organism. Overcoming habits requires repeated interventions and takes time. It is something that must be built up through determined effort and established through practice. Projects to develop practices and intellectual structures to manage such a process are being put into place, but they are in an early phase. Only those who can see the bigger picture and the more distant prospect will be able to give the project the energy it needs. Only those who can tolerate sustained exploration of the unconscious in all its forms of collectivity will be able to contribute fully to the project. In this, the West, with its long history of absorption and integration of the dynamics of the unconscious, has and will continue to play a unique role in our global advance for some time to come.

Ideas and Evolutionary Change

Mere ideas do not change us. Only ideas that we absorb and make part of ourselves can do that. When we absorb ideas, they become beliefs. Beliefs are what change us. Beliefs are ideas on which we are prepared to act. Our beliefs and consequent actions inform our engagement with people and the world around us. It is only through continually reexamining our beliefs and making serious efforts to live by them that we can realize our potentials and move forward on our evolutionary path, and it is only through the practice of our beliefs that we change.

Thus, *agape,* as a concept, has no power to change us. But if we absorb this concept so deeply that it becomes integral, something we feel in our bones, it can change how we interact socially and engage with the world. If we learn to act according to the feeling of *agape*, we change, and so do our lives. The process of making *agape* habitual occurs through the practice of *agape*. So, three steps are required to make *agape* an integrated part of us: 1) learning about *agape*, 2) developing our awareness of what *agape* feels like, and 3) practicing *agape* as a habitual part of our lives.

Transforming an idea, even a deeply felt idea, into a practice that informs all our actions and moral decisions is difficult. It takes time and determined effort. After all, to make such changes, we must overcome old, inadequate habits and replace them with new ones. A habit is an ingrained tendency to act in a certain way, and it cannot just be obliterated. A new habit must be substituted—in this case, a habit that reflects an agapic view of things. We must keep this in mind as we devise a strategy for enhancing *agape* in the world.

Happily, agapic love is already present within us as an instinct, ready to become manifest as felt experience. *Agape* is not merely an idea in the mind; it is a power we can sense within ourselves. We are not limited to learning about *agape* through the mind and its concepts; in fact, what we learn is useful largely for helping us to recognize blocks or impediments to *agape*'s natural exercise and finding ways to remove them. Beginning to practice *agape* initiates a kind of love therapy that helps us make agapically informed decisions. Learning about *agape*, whether through observation of the world around us, reading, discussing it with others, or noting its movement in our-selves, results in reflection about its practical place in our lives.

Because *agape* is natural or instinctual for us, learning to *feel agape* is not something we have to learn from the outside. We can feel it from the inside. And we actually *do* feel it—often—if not in its purest form then as a strong element of the *agape/eros* mix. There are ways to enhance and increase the frequency of *agape* in our lives. The simplest is to use the inherent ability we have to go inside, to become aware of our inner world, and explore things in our "inner theatre." This is what I have elsewhere called an *inner-mind trance*, a well-known example of which is a meditative state that seeks to explore the contents of the inner mind. The approach is simple. We settle into that inner world and then recall the times we have felt *agape,* particularly in its purest form, with little or no *eros* involved, evoking that golden vein of *agape* that we desire to inform our loving. It is a peculiarity of the inner-mind trance that when we recall experiences in the inner-mind state, we actually *re-experience* them or *re-feel* them. This re-living increases our ability to feel and apply *agape* in the various situations of our lives. It becomes a habit. The more often we do this, the better we love.

Over time, various great cultures have created communities dedicated to the enhancement of consciousness. In some of them, awareness of our inner and outer life of consciousness has been linked to practical action. What we need are communities seeking to find and apply full-bodied approaches that enable all three of the stages mentioned above: learning about *agape*, develop-ing the feeling of *agape*, and putting *agape* into practice. If *agape* is to be established in its true position of primacy in human moral life, and if *eros* is to be experienced and adapted into the evolutionary process, wherein *agape* holds its position of primacy, we need to develop more communities with powerful *agape* awareness.

Martin Luther King recognized this state of affairs and wrote about it in his first book, *Stride Toward Freedom*. His idea of *agape* was synonymous with that of Peirce:

> *Agape* means understanding, redeeming good will for all men. It is an overflowing love which is purely spontane-ous, unmotivated, groundless, and creative. It is not set in motion by any quality or function of its object. It is the

love of God operating in the human heart . . .. In the final analysis, *agape* means a recognition of the fact that all life is interrelated. All humanity is involved in a single process and all men are brothers . . .. Love, *agape*, is the only cement that can hold this broken community together. When I am commanded to love, I am commanded to restore community, to resist injustice, and to meet the needs of my brothers.[83]

The great spiritual teacher, Krishnamurti, said, "We do not change mankind by helping people, but by becoming loving."[84] We do not change people by providing them with a developmental scheme to follow. Rather, the world is transformed by our own unique personal transformation, carried out individually and in communities that encourage and embrace that transformation. Krishnamurti believed that if a person changes fundamentally, that person will affect the whole of humankind. Speaking of the development of benevolent love, he said, "Let a few of us work on this and we will change the world."

I agree with this view. We will get nowhere if we are caught in the depressing notion that we are all basically isolated units that affect each other from the outside. The truer picture is that humanity forms a dynamic interconnecting web of individual and communal nodes or personal centers. When one part of that web is transformed by love, the entire web benefits.

The transformation of the world involves the establishment of the primacy of agapic love in human relations, and all transformative practices must concentrate on this task. But the task must and will be carried out primarily on the level of community, as members test practices initiated by transformative communities of the past, continue those in existence, and plan those yet to come. This undertaking requires a sense of respect for past attempts and an attitude of experimentation and openness to innovations that will undoubtedly be discovered. The long-term project will involve a wise and effective winnowing of transformative practices to arrive at the most effective, a winnowing that is only in its early stages. I believe it is premature to make strong statements about how it is all going to settle out.

I have seen few examples of interpretive communities today that assist their participants through the three stages mentioned above. Only one of which I have personal knowledge seems to qualify in this regard. It is a network of communities devoted to what it calls Integral Transformative Practice, and its work is gradually being recognized internationally.[85] I am hopeful that many more such communities of practice exist, and I would be grateful if readers who know of other examples would inform me about them.

The Hard Solution

Some may be disappointed with the message of this chapter. They may wonder, "Where is the grand plan to defeat greed? Where is the proposal that, when put in place, will change everything?" What I propose is neither a grand plan nor a scheme to be applied from the top down. Grand plans cannot be put in place without preparation. The conditions that make grand plans cogent and ensure their durability must be created first. This is why the real solution to the problem of greed is the hard solution. The hard solution is this: Learn about, feel, and practice agapic love. It is a solution that requires hard work from us all. We have to prepare the way by changing ourselves, individually and collectively. We must go against the contemporary grain and surrender the notion that luminous ideas or dazzling schemes are the solution. Learning about agapic love is a hard part of the hard solution. Feeling agapic love is a hard part of the hard solution. Practicing agapic love is a hard part of the hard solution. Living *agape* and engaging everyone and everything agapically is the outcome of the hard solution. This cannot be a popular answer. It may be criticized as being too vague, as having unrealistic expectations, and for taking too long. I cannot say that such criticisms are without merit. I would like it to be easily laid out, easily carried through, and rapidly completed, but it is not, and cannot be, that simple. What I propose is the hard solution, but I am afraid it is also the only solution.

It is perhaps easy to see what it means to learn about *agape*. We have many resources for learning and deepening our grasp of its nature and operation. It may be a bit more difficult to get a sense of or feel *agape*. But this, too, is something that seems possible, because we all have a storehouse of remembered moments in which we have felt *agape* for others or the world, moments that were striking and left a lasting impression. We can find ways to recall and re-experience them. Describing what it means to practice *agape*, however, takes something more.

It helps to keep in mind that we are not always in a state of loving. There are great swaths of time during which we are operating from what Colin Wilson calls the "robot" in us,[86] doing things automatically and without intensity. Nevertheless, we find ourselves experiencing love more often that we may realize. If we are making a conscious decision to engage the world, to carry out some kind of action or another, we can be sure we are involved in an exercise of love. When we decide to take an action, there is likely a certain degree of intensity, and insofar as we love consciously, to that degree we take over from the robot. This state of deciding has a great range of intensity, however, from the low level of ordinary, commonplace, everyday decisions, to the higher feeling of a moment of crisis, to the highest excitement of a true creative breakthrough. We need a high degree of intensity, or focal concentration on something, to activate potentials that we have not actualized before, to bring the truly novel into the world. At such a point of intensity, we have shifted from seeing the world as familiar and ordinary to seeing it as strange, peculiar, and profoundly mysterious, and this experience is not at all comfortable. It is not just we ourselves who experience this perspective as uncomfortable; those who encounter us in this state may feel uncomfortable, too. We stir the pot of the world to some degree or another, and the resulting ripples change the world forever. For the most part, people do not want the world to change significantly. This is why to the degree that we maintain this sense of alienation, we are outsiders, in Wilson's meaning of the term.[87] When we find ourselves in a truly intense and at the same time alienated state, giving birth to a new perspective on things and activating some significant potentials, we are in the grips of the power of agapic love. We are moving not just ourselves but also the whole of creation along the path of evolutionary advance. The tie between *agape* and the evocation of potentials is so powerful that we might even say that the degree of purity of *agape* we experience may be measured by the degree of significant novelty and growth we produce. When we examine our discomfort, we realize that our most profound creative choices are almost totally devoid of desire, of *eros*.

So, the practice of *agape* involves constantly shifting out of being satisfied with a life of robotic response to the world and choosing intense engagement instead. It means deciding in more and more of the situations of our lives to take a stance of readiness to see the world and all that is in it as profoundly mysterious, an unfathomable source of potentials waiting to be realized. It is to overcome the fear of the new and the unfamiliar and to establish in its place the attitude of marveling at the sheer magnitude of the possibilities of evolutionary growth that show themselves all around. It is to take up the perspective of the outsider, but not in the sense of being isolated and alone— quite the contrary. Each of us will find a place as a localized, personal node in a seamless net of dynamic connections, all being urged forward on their evolutionary path and each of us doing our part as a conscious participant in making the world the greatest it can be.

Practice implies action. The practice of *agape* involves building up the habit of seeing how the world is animated by the universal presence and force of *agape*. Once we have experienced this perspective, we can, whenever and wherever we want, return our attention to it. This habitual act will gradually infuse our view of the events of our lives with the sense of agapic presence everywhere and influence all our practical decisions. The repeated renewal of the agapic vision is the practice of *agape*.

Epilogue:
A Personal Note on Optimism

I believe the hard solution will eventually bring success, and we will be able to identify progress as we go along. I feel optimistic about our chances, but I must admit that optimism is something of a natural disposition for me. In his introduction to my book, *Trance Zero*, Colin Wilson referred to my having a kind of natural cheerfulness and optimism, something he called "the secret life," a curious, deep glow inside that gives a person a sense of meaning and purpose. I believe this optimism exists in everyone, based as it is on the presence in us of the eternal force of *agape*.

The eventual installation of *agape* in a place of primacy in human affairs would mean a state of things that might seem startling to us, given that, in the present, we are surrounded by the dominance of greed. Directing agapic love to all, no matter how undeserving they may seem; seeing all people as brothers and sisters, not because they are of the same blood, the same clan, the same class, the same race, the same religion, or the same culture but because they are of the same human race; looking after our own evolutionary growth while at the same time encouraging that of all others; making moral decisions based on the primacy of *agape*, even at some personal cost; and, yes, even loving the sinner while hating the sin—is this too incredible to contemplate? The originators of the great spiritual and religious visions of the world did not think so. Neither do so many of the practitioners of the true spirit of these movements today. And neither do I.

I would like to conclude with what I believe is the true basis for optimism about the triumph of *agape* in the world: the fact that human *agape* is a participatory love. Although we experience ourselves loving agapically and acting on the basis of that love, human beings do not own *agape*. Nor does it depend on us for its existence. Rather, it is an enabling precondition, a prior state of affairs that was the essential foundation of the universe's coming into being and is the force driving its evolutionary advance. It existed before us, standing as it does at the universe's point of entry into concrete existence. And it will exist after us—if it turns out that there is an "after us." Our task, so to speak, is not to impose it on the world but to be agents of its evolutionary work, particularly in the conduct of human affairs.

Agape cannot be destroyed, for it stands indestructibly at the heart of the universe. It also exists in our hearts, and it is the most deeply embedded of all our instinctual feelings. True, its existence there is participatory and, therefore, subject to the vagaries of a free will that can act contrary to the primacy of *agape*. Nevertheless, if we fearlessly acknowledge life as it reveals itself to us, we are not forced into pessimism, but, on the contrary, must affirm that *agape* manifests constantly all around us. We must acknowledge it, even in the face of the defeats of *agape* in human social life that are such a source of consternation. The truth is, in the midst of all the divisions, conflicts, and oppositions, we are confronted with an abundance of agapic emotion and agapically inspired deeds every day, everywhere in the world. Our failure to give it primacy are so dramatic, so striking, that we might easily believe that *agape* has already lost the battle. This is not the case. Paradoxically, once we face without flinching the extensive inroads of destructive greed in the world, it becomes possible, perhaps for the first time, to see the enormous counter wave of *agape* manifesting in humanity's interactions not only with each other but also with the world of nature in which we are immersed. It is precisely because *agape* cannot be destroyed that I believe it will win out in the end. It is too central to evolution and too instinctive in us to fail. Although I agree with Peirce that there is no guarantee that the world will exist long enough for us to reach the ultimate outcome desired by our combined interpretive communities of inquiry—the primacy of *agape*—I also agree with his assertion that there is no definite proof to the contrary. The world's present state seems to be a temporary setback in the advance of love in the human community. Evolution does have its backwaters and failures, after all. It does not move steadily and inevitably from advance to advance, surging forward with unwavering progress to ultimate triumph. But even though we may have bad days now, I believe we have better days to which we can look forward. In the meantime, we can still have the satisfaction of experiencing personal and communal growth as we work together on our fitful path forward. It is *agape* that urges us and encourages us along the way.

Bibliography

Barbery, Muriel. *The Elegance of the Hedgehog*. Translated from the French by Alison Anderson. New York, NY: Europa Editions, 2008.

Corrington, Robert. *An Introduction to C. S. Peirce: Philosopher, Semiotician, and Ecstatic Naturalist*. Lanham, MD: Rowman & Littlefield, 1993.

———. *Ecstatic Naturalism: Signs of the World*. Bloomington: Indiana University Press, 1994.

———. *Nature's Sublime: An Essay in Aesthetic Naturalism*. Lanham, MD: Lexington Books, 2013.

Crabtree, Adam. "Mesmerism, Divided Consciousness and Multiple Personality." In *Franz Anton Mesmer und die Geschichte des Mesmerismus*, edited by Heinz Schott. Stuttgart: Franz Steiner, 1984.

———. "Explorations of Dissociation in the First Half of the Twentieth Century." In *Split Minds and Split Brains*, edited by Jacques Quen. New York, NY: New York University Press, 1986.

——— *Animal Magnetism, Early Hypnotism, and Psychical Research, 1766–1925: An Annotated Bibliography*. White Plains, NY: Kraus international Publications, 1988.

———. *From Mesmer to Freud: Magnetic Sleep and the Roots of Psychological Healing*. New Haven, CT: Yale University Press, 1993.

———*Trance Zero: Breaking the Spell of Conformity*. Toronto: Somerville House, 1997.

———. *Charles Sanders Peirce.* Website of the Esalen Institute. Big Sur, CA, 2010a. http://www.esalen.org/sites/default/files/resource_attachments/crabtree-peirce.pdf.

———. *Position Paper on Theory.* Website of the Esalen Institute. Big Sur, CA, 2010b. http://www.esalen.org/sites/default/files/resource_attach-ments/crabtree_position_paper_on_theory.pdf.

———. *Memoir of a Trance Therapist: Hypnosis and the Evocation of Human Potential.* Victoria, BC: Friesen Press, 2014.

———. "Continuity of Mind: A Peircean Vision." In *Beyond Physicalism: Toward Reconciliation of Science and Spirituality.* Edited by Edward Kelly, Adam Crabtree, and Paul Marshall. Lanham MD: Rowman & Littlefield, 2015.

Docherty, Thomas. *Universities at War.* Los Angeles, CA: Sage Swifts, 2015.

Ellenberger, Henri. *The Discovery of the Unconscious.* New York, NY: Basic Books, 1970.

Hare, Robert. *Without Conscience: The Disturbing World of the Psychopaths Among Us.* New York, NY: Guilford Press, 1999.

James, William. *Principles of Psychology, Vol. 1.* New York, NY: Henry Holt, 1890.

———. *The Will to Believe and Other Essays in Popular Philosophy.* New York, NY: Longmans, Green, 1897.

———. *Some Problems of Philosophy.* New York, NY: Longmans Green, 1911.

Jung, Carl. *The Symbolic Life, Vol. 18 of The Collected Works of C. G. Jung.* Translated by R. F. C. Hull. Princeton, NJ: Princeton University Press, 1977.

———. *The Archetypes of the Collective Unconscious,* Vol. 9, Pt. 1, *The Collected Works of C. G. Jung.* Translated by R. F. C. Hull. Princeton, NJ: Princeton University Press, 1980.

Kelly, Edward and Emily Kelly, with Adam Crabtree, Alan Gauld, Michael Grosso, and Bruce Greyson. *Irreducible Mind: Toward a Psychology for the 21st Century*. Lanham, MD: Rowman & Littlefield, 2007.

Kelly, Edward, with Adam Crabtree and Paul Marshall, eds. *Beyond Physicalism: Toward Reconciliation of Science and Spirituality*. Lanham, MD: Rowman & Littlefield, 2015.

King, Martin Luther Jr. *Strive Toward Freedom: The Montgomery Story*. New York, NY: Harper and Row, 1958.

Kripal, Jeffry. *Comparing Religions*. Oxford, UK: Wiley Blackwell, 2014.

Kruse, Felicia. "Nature and Semiosis." *Transactions* of the Charles S. Peirce Society 26, no. 2: 211–224, 1990.

Lachman, Gary. *Beyond the Robot: The Life and Work of Colin Wilson*. New York, NY: J. P. Tarcher, 2016.

Leonard, George. *The End of Sex: Love After the Sexual Revolution*. Los Angeles, CA: J. P. Tarcher, 1983.

Murdoch, Iris. *Bruno's Dream*. New York: Viking Press, 1969.

———. *An Unofficial Rose*. London: Vintage Books, 2000a.

———. *The Philosopher's Pupil*. London: Vintage Books, 2000b.

Nagel, Thomas. *Mind and Cosmos: Why the Materialist Neo-Darwinian Conception of Nature Is Almost Certainly False*. Oxford: Oxford University Press, 2012.

Nijinsky, Vaslav. *The Diary of Vaslav Nijinsky: Unexpurgated Edition*. Edited by Joan Acocella. New York, NY: Farrar, Straus, and Giroux, 1995.

Peirce, C. S. "Review of Clark University, 1889–1899." *Science*, New Series, 11, 620–621, 1900.

———. *The Collected Papers of Charles Sanders Peirce*, Vols. 1–6, 1931–1935, edited by Charles Hartshorne and Paul Weiss; Vols. 7–8, 1958, edited by A.W. Burks. Cambridge, MA: Harvard University Press, 1931–1958. Cited as: CP followed by volume number, a period, and the paragraph number (e.g., CP 4.24).

———. *The Essential Peirce: Selected Philosophical Writings*, Vol. 2. Edited by the Peirce Edition Project. Bloomington, IN: Indiana University Press, 1998.

Ventimiglia, Michael. "Evolutionary Love, in Theory and Practice." Doctoral thesis, 2001. Available: http://exordio.qfb.umich.mx/archivos%20 pdf%20de%20trabajo%20umsnh/aphilosofia/tesis%20nuevas/final-submission.pdf.

Wiley, Norbert. *The Semiotic Self.* Cambridge, UK: Polity Press, 2005.

Wilson, Colin. *The Outsider.* London, UK: Victor Gollancz, 1956.

———. *Mysteries.* London, UK: Hodder and Stoughton, 1978.

Index

Notes

1   CP 6.287. In line with the conventions of Peirce scholarship, citations in the form "CP *v.p.*" are used here to refer to Peirce's writings as they are set out in *The Collected Papers of Charles Sanders Peirce,* ed. Charles Hartshorne and Paul Weiss (Cambridge, MA: Harvard University Press, 1931–1958); *v* indicates the volume number, and *p* the paragraph number.

2   Adam Crabtree. *Memoir of a Trance Therapist* (Victoria, BC: Friesen Press), 2014; and "Continuity of Mind: A Peircean Vision*,"* in *Beyond Physicalism: Toward Reconciliation of Science and Spirituality*, ed. Edward Kelly, Adam Crabtree, and Paul Marshall (Lanham, MD: Rowman & Littlefield), 2015.

3   I owe this felicitous formulation of the delicate balance necessary in human love to Christina Grote.

4   CP 6.293–305.

5   CP 1.204.

6   See my paper at http://www.esalen.org/sites/default/files/resource_attachments/crabtree-peirce.pdf.

7   See Robert Corrington. *An Introduction to C. S. Peirce: Philosopher, Semiotician, and Ecstatic Naturalist* (Lanham, MD: Rowman & Littlefield), 1993, 179: "The potencies of nothingness are ontologically prior to the possibilities that obtain in what we could call the "Lesser" nothingness. Lesser nothingness is the domain of nothingness

of cosmic possibility and variety. This is a kind of storehouse of possible objects and events. Prior to the storehouse is the deeper tendency toward diversification that is not internal variety, but which will make variety possible."

8   Thomas Nagel, *Mind and Cosmos: Why the Materialist Neo-Darwinian Conception of Nature Is Almost Certainly False* (Oxford: Oxford University Press), 2012, 7.

9   CP 6.156–157.

10   See Corrington, *An Introduction to C. S. Peirce.*

11   CP 2.228.

12   CP 5.473.

13   CP 5.448 n.1.

14   C. S. Peirce, *The Essential Peirce: Selected Philosophical Writings*, ed. Peirce Edition Project. Bloomington, ID: Indiana University Press 1998, 2: 326.

15   See Felicia Kruse, "Nature and Semiosis," Transactions of the Charles S. Peirce Society 26, no. 2: 211–224, 1990.

16   CP 4.551.

17   Corrington, *An Introduction to C. S. Peirce*, 141.

18   MS 318, pp. 00205–00206, quoted in Corrington, *An Introduction to C. S. Peirce*, 163. This notion of universal semiosis can only be adequately explored in the context of Peirce's cosmology and his objective idealism. It is not possible to fully discuss those issues here. For a more detailed treatment, see Corrington, *Introduction to C. S. Peirce*, 75–166; and Kruse, "Nature and Semiosis."

19   Kruse, "Nature and Semiosis," 1990, 218–20.

20   Robert Corrington, *Ecstatic Naturalism: Signs of the World* (Bloomington, ID: Indiana University Press), 1994, 28.

21   Corrington *An Introduction to C. S. Peirce*, 159.

22   Iris Murdoch, *The Philosopher's Pupil* (London: Vintage Books), 2000, 124.

23   William James, *Principles of Psychology, Vol. 1.* (New York: Henry Holt), 1890, 448.

24   William James, *Some Problems of Philosophy* (New York: Longmans Green), 1911, 50–51.

25   James *Some Problems of Philosophy*, 5.

26   CP 1.135.

27   James, *The Will to Believe and Other Essays in Popular Philosophy* (New York: Longmans, Green) 1897, 68–69.

28   Nagel, *Mind and Cosmos*, 15.

29   Kelly et al., *Beyond Physicalism,* xii.

30   *Ibid.* xv.

31   *Ibid.*, xvi–xvii, xxii.

32   C.G. Jung, *The Archetypes of the Collective Unconscious,* Vol. 9, Pt. 1, *The Collected Works of C. G. Jung,* trans. R. F. C. Hull (Princeton, NJ: Princeton University Press), 1980, 282.

33   C.G. Jung, *The Symbolic Life,* Vol. 18, *The Collected Works of C. G. Jung,* trans. R. F. C. Hull. Princeton, NJ: Princeton University Press) 1977, 14–15.

34   Nagel, *Mind and Cosmos,* 7.

35   Peirce, MS 668, 16–17.

36   Peirce, MS 668, 16–17. For more about the "I" in Peirce, see Norbert Wiley, *The Semiotic Self* (Cambridge, UK: Polity Press), 2005.

37   CP 6.289.

38   Crabtree, *Memoir of a Trance Therapist.*

39   For a more detailed discussion of the narrative contained in this section, see Crabtree, *Memoir of a Trance Therapist.*

40   Crabtree, *Memoir of a Trance Therapist.*

41   See Adam Crabtree, *From Mesmer to Freud: Magnetic Sleep and the Roots of Psychological Healing* (New Haven, CT: Yale University Press), 1993; *Trance Zero: Breaking the Spell of Conformity* (Toronto: Somerville House), 1997; and *Memoir of a Trance Therapist.*

42   Vaslav Nijinsky, *The Diary of Vaslav Nijinsky: Unexpurgated Edition*, ed. Joan Acocella (New York, NY: Farrar, Straus, and Giroux), 1995.

43   Crabtree, *Trance Zero.*

44   Crabtree, *Memoir of a Trance Therapist.*

45   George Leonard, *The End of Sex: Love After the Sexual Revolution* (Los Angeles: J. P. Tarcher), 24–36.

46   Iris Murdoch, *An Unofficial Rose* (London: Vintage Books), 110.

47   In her book, *Bruno's Dream,* Iris Murdoch deftly describes the tortured inner moral dialogue of a man caught in the complexities of intertwined lives. After taking actions based largely on his own personal desires, he suddenly becomes aware of the possible destructive effects of his further decisions on the others involved. Here agapic concerns begin to come to the fore and greatly complicate matters. (See Iris Murdoch, *Bruno's Dream* (New York, NY: Viking), 1969, 186–90). 48   CP 6.290–292.

49   CP 6.289.

50   See Adam Crabtree, "Mesmerism, Divided Consciousness and Multiple Personality," in Franz Anton, *Mesmer und die Geschichte des Mesmerismus*, ed. Heinz Schott (Stuttgart: Franz Steiner), 1984; "Explorations of Dissociation in the First Half of the Twentieth Century," in *Split Minds and Split Brains*, ed. Jacques Quen (New York, NY: New York University Press), 1986; *Animal Magnetism, Early Hypnotism, and Psychical Research, 1766–1925: An Annotated Bibliography* (White Plains, NY: Kraus International Publications) 1988; *From Mesmer to Freud*; and *Memoir of a Trance Therapist*. See also Crabtree in Kelly et al., *Irreducible Mind: Toward a Psychology for the 21st Century* (Lanham, MD: Roman and Littlefield), 2007; and in Kelly et al., *Beyond Physicalism*.

51   Crabtree, *From Mesmer to Freud*, chapter 7.

52   Henri Ellenberger, *The Discovery of the Unconscious* (New York, NY: Basic Books), 1970.

53   Crabtree, *From Mesmer to Freud*, chapter 7.

54   Colin Wilson, *The Outsider* (London: Victor Gollancz), 1956. Colin Wilson developed this foundational idea in *The Outsider* and the five books that followed it. For a helpful view of the development of Wilson's thought, see Lachman 2016.

55   Robert Hare, *Without Conscience: The Disturbing World of the Psychopaths Among Us* (New York, NY: Guilford Press), 1999.

56   In this segment, I draw upon some key ideas developed by Robert Corrington in *Nature's Sublime: An Essay in Aesthetic Naturalism* (Lanham, MD: Lexington Books), 2013.

57   Corrington, *Nature's Sublime*, p. 89.

58   Glenn Gould interview by Alex Trebek, https://www.youtube.com/watch?v=1nZTgAGSajA.

59   Wilson, 1956.

60   Corrington, *Nature's Sublime*, pp. 90–91.

61   CP 6. 288.

62   The nearest thing I have seen to such a community is the Center for Theory and Research at Esalen, of which I have been privileged to be a part.

63   Jeffrey Kripal, *Comparing Religions* (Oxford: Wiley Blackwell), 94.

64   A pared-down list of the world's religions would be: polytheism, Judaism, Christianity, Islam, Hinduism, Sikhism, Buddhism, Daoism, Confucianism. Some say atheism should be included on this list, but I disagree. Although it has own creed based on faith and a literature that serves as the basis for proselytizing, it lacks rituals and social institutions as well as the belief in some power that is radically other or more.

65   CP 6.289.

66   C.S. Peirce, "Review of Clark University, 1889–1899," *Science,* New Series 11, 1900): 620.

67   Ibid.

68   Ibid.

69   Thomas Docherty, *Universities at War* (Los Angeles, CA: Sage Swifts), 2015, back cover.

70   For more on the pros and cons of tenure, see the *Wall Street Journal* article at http://www.wsj.com/articles/SB10001424052702303610504577418293114042070.

71   CP 6.288.

72   Peirce, "Review of Clark University," 621.

73   Barbery 2008.

74   Kripal, *Comparing Religions,* p. 11.

75   CP 8.81.

76   CP 7.571 and 572.

77   CP 7.574–576.

78   CP 7.572.

79   CP 2. 654.

80   CP 6.288.

81   Crabtree, *Trance Zero*.

82   Wilson, *The Outsider*.

83   Martin Luther King Jr., *Strive Toward Freedom: The Montgomery Story* (New York, NY: Harper and Row), 1958, 104–6.

84   Iris Murdoch and Jiddu Krishnamurti, Brockwood Park, Dialogue 2, 1984 https://www.youtube.com/watch?v=_-9fsZW_OZI.

85   Integral Transformative Practice website. http://www.itp-international.org.

86   Colin Wilson, *Mysteries* (London: Hodder and Stoughton), 1978, 34.

87   Wilson, *The Outsider*.

About the Author

Adam Crabtree is the author of books on hypnosis and the history of psychotherapy and dissociative disorders, such as multiple personality. He is on the faculty of the Centre for Training in Psychotherapy, Toronto.

CPSIA information can be obtained
at www.ICGtesting.com
Printed in the USA
BVHW01*0724200218
508119BV00007B/196/P